ICY PLEASURES

MINNESOTA CELEBRATES WINTER

ICY PLEASURES

MINNESOTA CELEBRATES WINTER

Paul Clifford Larson

Afton Historical Society Press
Afton, Minnesota

To Pam, who smiles in the winter
but laughs in the spring

Library of Congress Cataloging-in-Publication Data
Larson, Paul Clifford.
    Icy pleasures : Minnesota celebrates winter / Paul
Clifford Larson.
      p.   cm.
    Includes bibliographical references and index.
    ISBN 1-890434-01-9
    1. Winter sports—Minnesota.   I. Title.
GV840.7.U6L37   1997
796.9 09776—dc21   97-25217
                                CIP

Printed in Canada

Half title page photo: Winners of the Decorated Sled contest in the 1926 Duluth Winter Frolic
Frontispiece photo: 1992 St. Paul ice castle at night

The Afton Historical Society Press is a non-profit organization that takes
great pride and pleasure in publishing fine books on Minnesota subjects.

W. Duncan MacMillan, president   *Patricia Condon Johnston,* publisher

Afton Historical Society Press
P.O. Box 100
Afton, MN 55001
1-800-436-8443

CONTENTS

PREFACE

Since the turrets of St. Paul's first ice palace pierced the frosty air in 1886, Minnesota has been a state renowned as much for its celebrations of winter as for those winters themselves. Other areas of the United States may be more prone to blizzards or equally suitable for ice palaces. But none couples a reputation for ferocious winters with so rich a history of outdoor sports events and festivals, each vigorously embracing the worst that the season has to offer.

Until the great St. Paul carnivals of the 1880s, the flowering of organized winter entertainments took place with the halting progress natural to so vulnerable an affair. Some of the component sports evolved from practices that nobody thought to be particularly amusing. The snow "train" pulled by dogs was a clumsy, crudely fashioned wood sled for hauling equipage, provisions, and mail; few considered pitting dogsleds against each other in public contests, and no one could have imagined the train itself, a plank with its front curled up, raging through the ranks of northern society as a gravity-propelled vehicle called the toboggan. Snowshoes were an interesting French trapper adaptation of a mode of American Indian winter travel but nothing for the "better class" of people to trouble themselves with. Even skiing was little more than a curiosity, a peculiar Norwegian way of getting about on an impossibly skinny sort of snowshoe. Ice fishing, that most notorious of Minnesota pastimes, added variety to a weary winter diet of grains and salted meat; nobody could have mistaken it for a good time.

Quite apart from odd or stressful activities that had not yet been elevated to recreational status, bona fide winter sports were slow to catch on in what was still largely pioneer territory. The ice-skating clubs that took New England by storm in the 1860s left many Minnesotans out in the cold, for they required society as well as water to form a substantial upper crust. When the roller-skating fad of the 1880s began to lure hardy northerners into buildings, skating on ice nearly lapsed into a piece of nostalgia for the hardier days gone by. Curling, an ancient Scottish pastime, languished for nearly thirty years in Minnesota as an isolated and eccentric entertainment, its sole participants a small band of men in a tiny rural community who took to the rink between readings of Bobby Burns's poetry.

St. Paul's winter carnivals brought together all of these frigid activities for the first time. Their vaunted purpose was to combat eastern ridicule of the state's supposedly Siberian conditions. But the carnival activities also had a profound impact on how Minnesotans themselves behaved in the winter. The toboggan craze descended from Canada into the United States the very year St. Paul organized its first winter carnival, and that carnival became the primary vehicle for the spread of the sport — and of sporting associations in general — throughout the state. Snowshoeing became the essence of winter sociability in towns from Crookston to Rochester. Dog sledding, now enjoying a revival through much of Canada and the northern states, was an integral part of the Indian and French voyageur exhibits at the early carnivals and made headlines in the 1916 and 1917 editions. A strong push from the first carnivals propelled curling into the limelight as the most popular of all winter competitions, where it remained until hockey pushed it aside between the world wars. Thousands of Minnesotans also got their first glimpse of skiing at winter carnival exhibitions.

St. Paul has long ceased to be the epicenter of cold-weather activity in Minnesota, as winter sports events and festivals have dispersed throughout the northern half of the state. In addition, the tobogganing, curling, skating, and skiing exhibitions and competitions that were once the heart of winter carnivals everywhere have either lapsed in popularity, found more effective venues, or retired from Minnesota altogether. In their place has arisen a new array of activities, this time originating in communities with their own agendas, none of which includes allegiance to St. Paul or even to their own winter carnival histories.

The orientation of my research has been historical throughout, its scope confined largely to the years before World War II. Postwar editions of the St. Paul carnival have received relatively short shrift, and references to later festivals have been included only to indicate the new directions being taken by current winter celebrations. I had intended to give these latter more consideration, but they proved far too abundant to bring under the historical umbrella. A full account of the many thriving winter festivals in the state today would be another book.

In spite of considerable promotional activity, the birth of each Minnesota winter celebration has tended to be a profoundly local affair. When I set out to discover and document them, I assumed that there was a network of memories, traditions, and communications among the various towns that have drawn up slates of winter activities. As it turns out, nothing could be further from the truth. Photographs of the countless outstate winter sports frolics of the Depression era have barely found their way into public collections, in spite of well-publicized snapshot taking at many of them. For over a hundred years publicists for winter festivals everywhere have spouted claims of introducing a new event, hosting the largest crowds, or being the only

regional venue for a sport when the most casual glance at the historical record or the current newspapers of other towns shows otherwise. Even today, organizers of modern dog-sled racing and cross-country skiing events trace their roots to Canada and Scandinavia directly, rather than through the many St. Paul winter carnivals and Iron Range frolics that featured them.

All of these various disconnections within and among local winter celebrations pose difficulties for the researcher, but more importantly they also testify to how widespread and independent the spirit of winter celebration has become in Minnesota. Carnival organizers have focused on the needs and aspirations of their own community or, just as often, on the fantasies borne of informal discussions among friends and the workings of their own imaginations. As fads change or interests wane, even those festivals that begin to be hallowed by tradition are forced to reinvent themselves or fade into the oblivion of newspaper morgues and microfilms.

That the history of circumstances so quickly changed and events so haphazardly documented can be brought to light at all owes a great deal to the spirited reportage of local newsmen. Since the days of the territory, newspaper editors and reporters have shamelessly promoted Minnesota's winter climate, the hardiness of its people, and the sports that thrive in glacial conditions. They have also chronicled in the most minute detail not only the great public events of the winter but also each small stirring of the season from snowshoe tramps to turkey shoots. Above all, the best of them have couched their observations in language that crackles with hyperbole, mind-twisting metaphor, flights of eloquence and erudition, and the driest of humors. Nineteenth-century journalists in particular so understood and exulted in their role as myth makers that their language itself compels us to doubt the predominant mythology of our own day, in which a thermometer reading seventy-two degrees Fahrenheit and an electronic image of someone else enjoying the winter have become icons of the good life.

This book could not have been written without the vast collection of historical images that have been donated to the Minnesota Historical Society since the beginnings of photography in the state. To those individuals and organizations wise enough to know that what they did and recorded held value for those who came after, and to the organization that has preserved their gifts, I owe a primary debt of thanks. The MHS research library staff has been particularly helpful in permitting me to sort through an enormous universe of material in order to create that single small constellation of photographs that comprise this book. They have also pointed the way to many an arcane or curiously filed resource that ended up providing nuance and texture to the work.

To flesh out the St. Paul winter carnivals, I have had the good fortune of browsing the archives of the St. Paul Festival and Heritage Foundation. Programs assistant Jennifer Eyrich was particulary helpful in pointing the way and authorizing the use of many of the wonderful images from that collection. I am also grateful to numerous staff members and volunteers of the Ramsey County Historical Society, the Hennepin County Historical Society, the Minneapolis Public Library, and the St. Paul Public Library in helping me to locate and copy archival photographs unique to each of those institution's collections.

Pat Maus, curator of manuscripts for the Northeast Minnesota Historical Center in Duluth, provided splendid pictures of the Duluth Winter Frolics and opened the door to my discovery of the proliferation of winter carnivals on the Iron Range during the Great Depression. Bud Gazelka, photo archivist of the Iron Range Interpretive and Research Center, found some rare images of Laskienen events and local snow sculptures, and Wanda Hoyum, executive director of the Beltrami County Historical Society, was kind enough to send me information and superb pictures from the amazing Paul Bunyan Winter Carnival. Successive directors of the Pope County Historical Society combed little-used files for invaluable information about early skiing activity in the Glenwood area and provided me with early photographs.

I also wish to thank those many directors, reporters, or chroniclers of current winter celebrations in towns throughout the northern half of the state who responded to my requests for information. Bill and Gloria Miller, the tireless organizers of the Voyageur Winter Festival in Ely, Ken Bresley, irrepressible co-inventor of Walker's Eelpout Festival (and much of its lore), Paul E. Nye, editor of Walker's *Pilot-Independent* and its misbegotten child, the *Pout-Independent,* Greg Cannell, guiding light of the Northwest Angle Winterfest, Ione Tomasetti, executive director of the Chisholm Chamber of Commerce, Charlotte McDermott of the Grand Rapids Wintersloss, and staff of the Kanabec County Historical Society, where the Vasaloppet is held, were especially generous with their time. I regret that I was able to incorporate so little of what they and many others shared with me within the bounds of the present book.

Sally Rubinstein subjected the text to her usual close editorial scrutiny, plucking it out of many a verbal quagmire and providing hope that I may yet solve the mysteries of comma and hyphen placement. As publisher, Patricia Johnston has been a constant source of encouragement and at crucial points a better judge than I of what might interest an audience larger than devout Minnesotans. Finally, to my wife Pamela I owe the gift of an express curiosity vigorous enough to raise hopes that other readers may enjoy the trek through Minnesota's winter celebrations as much as I.

To the wise, life is a festival.
RALPH WALDO EMERSON

THE CULT OF COLD

I NEVER KNEW WHAT COLD WEATHER WAS BEFORE

For a century and a half, Minnesota's winters have exercised the descriptive powers of all breeds of writers. Reporters, diarists, humorists, and historians have by this time fairly exhausted the resources of the English language on the subject. The image of Minnesota as a land of endless snow and bristling cold invariably grips the minds of outsiders — and even some of the faint-hearted among its own citizenry — with the tenacity of religion or, better yet, the haunting presence of a really well-told, scary story. How that image originated and became fixed in the public imagination is one of the main historical backdrops to the story of Minnesota's long history of winter celebrations.

Fort Snelling was the first permanent white settlement in what became the state of Minnesota, and the letters and reports that emanated from its early, lonely occupants quite naturally laid the foundation for the state's wintry notoriety. The first winter of 1819-20 was a shock to nearly all of the fort's inhabitants, many of whom knew snow as little more than a rare and delightful diversion. But that experience was nothing

St. Anthony Falls during a cold snap, ca. 1875

organization as a territory, achieved on March 3, 1849, waited more than a month for the river to break up so that a packet boat could plow through.[4]

Extreme conditions also greeted the first settlers in St. Anthony, a village upstream that would ultimately be absorbed into Minneapolis. After a warm and nearly cloudless October and November in 1850, winter came in with a vengeance, dropping temperatures to thirty degrees below zero in the first week of December. The depth and suddenness of the freeze created treacherous conditions on the Mississippi River as it froze over, sealing the village off from its only connection to other communities.[5]

On the strength of these and sundry other tales of winter hardship, all duly reported and repeated back east, New Englanders increasingly regarded Minnesota Territory as an American Siberia, as cold as it was remote. In point of fact, Minnesota conceived as a piece of the arctic wedged into an otherwise reasonably temperate country was a myth. By the time statehood was achieved in 1858, Minnesotans had accumulated enough comparative annual weather data to realize that the state's supposedly arctic status was exaggerated. Deep snowfalls were more common in upstate New York than in the Twin Cities. During the first decades of white settlement the total midwinter precipitation recorded at Fort Snelling averaged less than a fourth of that in the major cities of Maine, Vermont, and New Hampshire.[6] Temperatures, in the meantime, varied considerably from the north to the south of the state, a fact that argued against the common New England acceptance of the state's lowest readings (which invariably made eastern news) as its norm for any particular day.

But popular perceptions of the world's regions and peoples have never had much to do with statistical display or scientific argument. Like all good myths, they take a smattering of remarkable episodes as indications of a fundamental, underlying reality. Everyone knows that Frenchmen are great lovers, Italians are born singers, and Minnesotans spend five months of the year in a tomb of snow.

compared to what awaited them in February and March 1826. With winter expected to be on the way out, successive blizzards added two to three feet of snow to the existing accumulation. A windstorm on March 20 whipped up drifts as high as fifteen feet. As a final blow, a fierce thunderstorm on April 10 blew in not the proverbial showers but yet another blizzard with temperatures plummeting to just above the zero degree mark. April 21 arrived before the stretch of the Mississippi River below the fort began to clear of ice.[3]

Cold even more than snow dramatized the isolation of the Fort Snelling outpost, many miles removed from its supply post in Prairie du Chien, Wisconsin. Letters such as Jarvis's (quoted above) were typical of communications out of the fort in January. As late as 1849, brutal winter weather so long delayed the dog train delivering the news that by the time it arrived "the good people in the country below had forgotten all about it." News of Zachary Taylor's election as president arrived in January; even word of Minnesota's

Periodic winter snows of truly legendary pro-portions arrived just often enough to lend credence to the vision of Minnesota as a glacier somehow detached from the arctic shield, and journalists were quick to pick up on them. Newspaper editors throughout the state reveled in the worst of the storms, tabulating their ranking in the state's — or the nation's — recorded history of winter disasters and reciting the number of railroad lines blockaded, school children marooned, and frozen corpses discov-ered. In the limited world of the prairie journalist, this was probably as much news as his fledgling communi-ty had to offer in January or February, and he was simply making the most of it. But to the eastern read-er, where the horrors were inevitably communicated, this was not simply news to fill a winter gap; it was *the* word from Minnesota.

In the days before World War I, when the ground-work was laid for all but the most recent winter cele-brations in the state, three snowy cataclysms stood out from the rest. The first was a blizzard in January 1873, the second a long and vicious winter of perpetual snowfall in 1881, and the third a deep snow followed by gales in February 1909. Each made its own distinct contribution to the chilling litany of winter travail and triumph.

Local journalists labeled the blizzard of 1873 the "most severe snow storm ever known in the north-west," and if the qualification were made "since Min-nesota statehood," they were probably correct. After assuring his readers from other parts that "we don't have much weather in Minnesota," a writer for the *St. Paul Pioneer* launched into a horrendous descrip-tion. The storm began on the Tuesday afternoon of January 7, with the wind reaching "the velocity of a hurricane" by midnight and continuing with falling temperatures through the next day. No man, woman, or animal was safe outside who "could not breathe snow rather than air." All travel in and out of St. Paul ceased, although on Wednesday twelve students man-aged to make their way to Adams School near down-town, out of its usual attendance of five hundred.[7]

The real horrors of the storm fell on the outstate residents to the south and west of St. Paul on whom the blizzard "commenced without the shadow of warning and continued for sixty hours." A St. Paul train bound for Sioux City, Iowa, reached the prairie north of St. Peter before a snow blockade forced it to stop. Nineteen passengers spent the night aboard while the conductor sought out the nearest settle-ment. He secured a sleigh and provisions in Ottawa the next morning, and his passengers were saved. Teachers and students of country schools were simi-larly marooned. During his Tuesday night ordeal, that same conductor stumbled into a school still in session, with many parents who had arrived to take their children home forced to stay on through the night with them.

What made the 1873 blizzard particularly danger-ous — and ripe for myth — was its suddenness. Tuesday morning opened mild and sunny, offering promise of a January thaw. Hundreds of winter-weary farmers and laborers put on light clothes and pursued long-neglected tasks as if spring were due that after-noon. In the rural community of Windom, not far from the Iowa border, twenty-five teams of horses pulled into town for supplies and casually left for home; at the tiny station of Lincoln, fourteen railroad workers bid the train good-bye for the day, leaving their overcoats in the caboose. Then the snow began to fall, the winds driving it with such fury that "the sun seemed to entirely withdraw its light, and soon an almost impenetrable darkness settled over the earth." Houses were barely visible from across the street, and roads disappeared altogether. Teams of horses were discovered the next day covered by snow and frozen solid, the owner nearby or still in the seat. On Friday, one of the railroad workers was discovered three miles from the station, where he had fallen from exhaustion and died in his thin blue shirt.[8]

A northeastern Iowa photographer, Arthur McKay of Decorah, was among the first to capitalize on the commercial potential of storied midwestern blizzards. As soon in 1873 as the tracks were clear and the weather permitted, he hauled his gear to sites along railway lines to capture scenes of drifts as high as the trains, then sold the prints as stereopticon slides. Across the border, most Minnesota photographers still clung to the comfort of their studios. Where commercial photographs were taken, as at the Falls of St. Anthony, their purpose served artistic rather than documentary purposes. Local newspapers also failed to provide illustrations. Their figural engravings, like those of newspapers everywhere, were largely confined to tiny standardized cuts illustrating houses, miscellaneous commodities, and ornaments suitable for advertisements.

To grab the reader's eye — and national attention — editors and reporters had to resort to other graphic means. One of the commonest devices was the stacked headline, which followed a simple head with phrases spelling out the sensational content of the article to follow, each highlighted by a different type face. The editor of the *St. Paul Pioneer* was a master of the art, and his headlining of the blizzard of 1873 was one of his better efforts. "The Late Storm" at the top teases the reader's eye down through eight subheads culminating in a smallpox panic and a death from freezing. Stacked headlines such as this were the closest the nineteenth-century newspaperman could come to the grisly wirephotos of the twentieth century.

By 1880 pictures of natural disasters had achieved enough nationwide commercial potential that market-

Frozen foam on the Red Lake River, Red Lake Falls, ca. 1892

ing prints of them was an enterprise assured of quick profits. Minnesota weather immediately obliged with a winter that topped all its recorded predecessors, beginning with a heavy snowfall in October, continuing through nearly three feet of snow in November, and winding up in early March with storms that brought the season total to twelve and a half feet. Like the winter that culminated in the blizzard of 1873, it was also a time of racking cold, the mean temperature for the season sitting below ten degrees.[9]

When the first spring thaw arrived, commercial photographers swarmed out of their studios to capture dramatic views of the winter for national consumption. The most ambitious among them, Charles A. Tenney of Winona, published fifty-nine different stereopticon slides under the title "Minnesota Snow View Series of 1881." Although taken when the snow pack was already on the way down, these photographs brought a Minnesota winter directly before the eyes of any who owned a stereopticon. Among the most popular subjects was the roof of a railroad passenger car photographed from a snow bank above, making the car appear to be a casket lowered into its grave.

Compelling as such photographs might be, the camera was still not able to record anything of the great snowstorms but their aftermath. Film speed was too slow and conditions too uncomfortable to permit the photographer to set up and shoot while the storm was in progress. Conveying a sense of the storms in all their ferocity still fell to journalists, who by this time were regularly aided by skilled illustrators. In the prolonged winter of 1880-81, the editor of the *St. Paul and Minneapolis Pioneer Press* (into which the *Pioneer* had evolved) saved his best work until the end, when he could march the reader through tables of impressive statistics and a gazetteer of Minnesota railroad towns and their winter histories. Many of the town reports were obviously included to reinforce the writer's general themes that Minnesota winters are not nearly so bad as those in New England, that even the exceptional past winter caused no real suffering, and that such inconveniences as arose on the rail lines

could have been forestalled by snow fences. But for all his circumspection, the editor could not keep a certain chilling reality from creeping in; Lake City reported (from *southern* Minnesota) that the winter had brought forty-seven days of below zero temperatures, Brownton and Bird Island stations were without trains for sixty days, and several towns reported two to three feet of snow still on the ground near the end of March.

The very fact that so little blockading had occurred on rail lines could only add to the myth of Minnesotans having some peculiar affinity for deep snow. Only hundreds of miles of scientifically arranged snow fences and the invention of train plows prevented other communities from sharing the fate of Brownton and Bird. The ferocious winter of 1880-81 inspired *Harper's Weekly*

A lake shore after an ice storm near Worthington in December 1896

to send one of its artists, Charles Graham, to Minnesota and Dakota to show readers what winter railroad travel in the Northwest was supposed to look like. His featured engraving, published on January 27, 1883, illustrated a train driving full-throttle through a blizzard, thanks to a gargantuan plow attached to the front of the engine. A battery of smaller pictures invested this vision of the northwestern winter with true tabloid histrionics: wolves howl in the distance, stranded passengers call on the denizen of a log cabin for food, and visitors approach the train by snowshoe.

Several severe winters followed on the heels of the storied arctic blasts of 1880–81, and these gave way to successive winters with wild swings in weather, from autumnal conditions in December and January to

17

PASSENGERS CALLING ON A SETTLER FOR FOOD.

"Winter Railroad Travel in the Northwest." Popular illustrator Charles Graham depicted travel conditions in Minnesota and Dakota Territory for a national readership in *Harper's Weekly*

"Fun for the Boys," children jumping off a cattle car into a snow drift near Sleepy Eye on January 30, 1909

dramatic drops in temperature followed by sudden, short-lived snow storms. All of these made for an occasional hair-raising tale and some overly ripe journalism. Only a single other winter before World War I made so substantial a contribution to the state's weather lore, and that was the one that brought the blizzard of February 1909. What made this particular storm stand out from its predecessors was the monstrous drifting of the snow, particularly in the southern part of the state.

The year 1909 became the year of the winter photograph in Minnesota. Snapshooters in the southern half of the state captured image after image of buried or half-buried vehicles, buildings, and telegraph poles. More popular than even these subjects was a fascinating steam-engine attachment known as the rotary plow. Introduced into the Northwest in 1887, its

18

great advantage over the conventional train plow was its ability to propel snow away from the head of the train by means of numerous scoops arranged in concentric circles. It was a stunning piece of modern engineering, both in appearance and effect. One writer called it "one of the most beneficial triumphs of human skill which have blessed the nineteenth century" and assured the residents of isolated northern settlements that its advent would "strip winter of all its terrors." After the blizzard of 1909, communities across the southern half of the state published photographic postcards illustrating the rotary plow in local use, often with townspeople clustered around it with all the pride of tourists posing before the Eiffel Tower.[10]

Not to be outdone by what was happening below them, northern Minnesotans in 1909 found their own winter postcard subject. Spared the worst winds of the blizzard, logging camps actually profited from the heavy snowpack. One postcard after another showed mammoth loads of logs being pulled to the river or sawmill. It became a contest of superlatives, with each camp claiming its load to be the banner load, or the monster load, or the largest load ever hauled in the Northwest. The impracticality of such heavy loads was beyond question; their achievement was clearly, in the winter of 1909, a sport.

For all the pictorial possibilities of Minnesota's fiercest winters, newspaper writers and local boosters realized from the beginning the folly of making too much of them. From the 1860s onward, the worst weather was increasingly described as utterly exceptional, as if in a most inexplicable way Canada had furtively crept across its boundary. When the snow was deepest, it was flatteringly compared to the damp and dreary Decembers of the East Coast.

But the most realistic of these boosters realized that they could not hold a pen against the gale of New England prejudice. This was a battle they could not win. Devoutly insisting on the tolerability of Minnesota winters was no help, as it could easily be construed as one more instance of a Minnesotan showing

how inured he was to the hellish conditions of his life through five months of the year. So it fell to local journalists and boosters to romanticize the myth rather than dispel it. The various moral and literary forms of that romance developed into a second backdrop for the eventual enactment of Minnesota winter festivals.

The rotary steam snow shovel and some local residents in Sleepy Eye in January 1909

A typical "Banner Load" postcard from 1909

BANNER LOAD, PINE ISLAND, MINN., 1909.

Largest load of logs ever hauled on sleighs by horses.   50,580 ft.; 250 tons @ 9 carloads.   15 mile haul by six horses at J. A. Irvine & Co's Camp for Thief River Falls Lumber Co., Pine Island, Beltrami County, Minn., March 4, 1909.

Phil. McManamin, Foreman.   Jas. Crotty, Teamster.   Chas. Harmon and Tom Morgan, Loaders.   E. H. Moore, Scaler.

L. H. Halverson, Photographer, Blackduck, Minn.

THE HEALTHIEST REGION IN THE KNOWN WORLD

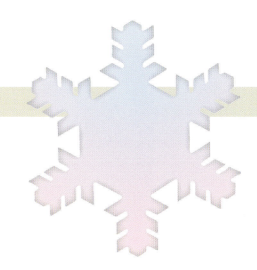

On a raw and cloudy spring day in 1849, James M. Goodhue, New Hampshire native and Amherst College graduate, arrived in St. Paul to found Minnesota's first newspaper. Ten days later, on April 28, the baptismal number of the *Minnesota Pioneer* trumpeted his new home's advantages to all who would read it. As Goodhue peered through his office window, he could see little to boast of other than piles of building material "scattered everywhere in admirable confusion." But credentials of a less tangible sort were already in place, and he spared no words bringing them forward. St. Paul was propitiously located at the head of steamboat navigation on the Mississippi River, where "bilious fevers and the ague were strangers." The young settlement was already that triumphant anomaly, a healthful town on the Mississippi. And the primary reason was its "salubrious" climate, not the least of whose virtues was a long, cold winter.[2]

Goodhue's vision of St. Paul and, by extension, most of Minnesota Territory as a refuge from disease stopped short of featuring winter weather, but it became increasingly

"**We hazard nothing in asserting that Minnesota is The Healthiest Region in the Known World.**"

DORR AND CUMMINGS, land agents, St. Anthony, Minnesota, 1856[1]

"**Every time you go out into the pure, cold atmosphere you are braced up anew. It is like the invigoration of champagne without the penalty of subsequent lassitude.**"

NORTHWEST ILLUSTRATED MONTHLY MAGAZINE, February 1888

[facing page]
Lunch time on a winter outing in 1926

plain to him and other regional boosters that snow and ice were the principal instruments of St. Paul's delivery from disease. Humans could survive a Minnesota winter, but their most noxious inflictions could not. Swamps froze to the base in January, and the agents of cholera, scarlet fever, diphtheria, and the flu were believed — with some claim to the truth — to freeze with them. The great ravages of the human body had, like the armadillo, halted their northern march somewhere just below the Iowa border.

Acknowledgment that not even germs cared to live here was not quite the most effective of advertisements for the territory, but Goodhue was just getting started. He had arrived in St. Paul as one of the fiercest winters known to white settlers was breaking up. Rather than dwelling on the cheerlessness of that long and tedious season, however, he claimed that it forcibly reminded him of a beautifully drawn winter scene of the Latin poet Horace and proceeded to quote a stanza. He even found solace in Horace's suggestion, "lignum super foco, large reponans" (wood on the hearth, constantly replenished). If winter put a halt to physical enterprise, it apparently also moved the human spirit to poetry, or at least to the memory of schoolboy Latin.[3]

Declarations of what Minnesota and its winters could do for the health of the human body were but the first step of a platform that would soon rise to the ethereal heights of spiritual well being. In September, with freezing weather again in the wings, Goodhue wrote a scathing indictment of those who failed to warm to his chosen state's wintry climate. Addressing it "To Farmers of the United States and Canada," his particular target was those who had "taken it into their brains that no part of this great globe is habitable, by reason of the cold, to a higher degree of latitude than about forty degrees north." After mocking them for preferring to "shiver about in thin sleezy garments" in a "hermaphrodite region, half tropical and half frigid," he turned to the wiser lot "who have been invigorated by the cold."

Goodhue's own New Hampshire stock was, of course, the paradigm, that "hard-fisted Yankee" who "to win a little field among the [stone] ledges outlives two or three generations of Suckers, who settle down on the fertile bottoms of the Illinois, amid vast savannas of Indian corn." In Minnesota, nature would not so spoil her children, for the "length of winter and invigorating climate invite man to exercise." In a rousing final metaphor, Goodhue absorbed his more sedate April advertisement into his full-chested vision of the true Minnesota resident. The Minnesotan "has a good boiler in him and steam to work off; while your Sucker is like one of the little old aguish steamboats that ran on the Illinois river seventeen years ago."[4]

By the time Goodhue directly encountered his first Minnesota January, his enthusiasm had levitated so far above his skin temperature that winter entombment itself became a garden of delight. On January 2, 1850, he reported in an almost confessional tone that the thermometer had recently read lower than twenty-eight degrees below zero, "but we dare not say how much." That shivering disclosure, however, was carefully sandwiched between the joyous reports that a foot of snow had brought good sleighing and that the clear sky and hushed atmosphere offered "the most lovely moonlight scenery ever beheld." In the same issue Goodhue avowed it to be "proverbial that St. Petersburgh [sic] and the capitals of other cold countries are the gayest places in the world during the reign of winter. The festivities and hilarity of our town on New Year's day confirm the truth, that cold weather

James Goodhue, ca. 1850, from a crayon drawing

22

can never freeze warm hearts. Saint Paul was yesterday swarming with animated fashion."[5]

To do the newspaperman justice, these various glorifications of his city's wintry virtues were widely scattered among much longer discourses on local events and political issues. But they captured in a nutshell the evolving package of cold weather themes that soon became mainstays of the territory's and state's self-promotion. Basking in the draftless warmth of a modern home or office, watching cable television above a fishing hole cut through the carpet of the latest icehouse, or shopping in the "downtown without weather" afforded by the skyway system leaves the modern Minnesotan with little sense today of how far pioneering spirits had to stretch in order to draw pleasure from their icy solitude. After Goodhue's ecstatic outbursts, more than a generation passed before the first winter festival was planned, the first lake colonized with ice houses, the first ski club organized, or the first dog-sled run taken that was officially fun.

If the flowering of a generalized Minnesota euphoria over winter took place slowly, it was not for want of hype. Goodhue had anticipated the major themes: (1) cold is healthful, (2) cold is energizing and uplifting, and (3) cold is fun. These three themes were served to the resident public and the potential immigrant in language as deliciously excessive as the architecture and the apparel of the day.

The theme of Minnesota's great health benefits drew the most persistent and long-winded support of the three. In 1856, the village of St. Anthony published one of the earliest tracts to extol the health-giving quality of local winters. Written as a guide to the territory by an anonymous "old resident, " it opined that the dryness of the air was the cause of "the peculiar salubrity of the climate of Minnesota. Our bracing, invigorating atmosphere operates as a tonic and stimulant on the system." As a result, winters were far more pleasant as well as less harmful to the human system. An incidental benefit, offered without example or elaboration, was that "mud is almost unknown in Minnesota." To prove that his

opinion was not simply local boosterism, the writer excerpted lengthy passages from an address by a Chicago newspaper editor. According to the impartial Mr. Scripps, "the atmosphere is dry beyond belief." Apparently the benefit increased northward, for the upper reaches of Minnesota were referred to as "the healthy part of the Territory."[6]

Ten years later, after the territory had become a state, the Minnesota commissioner of immigration

Summer vacationers at the Winslow House in St. Anthony, ca. 1865. Far and away the largest and most elegantly appointed hostelry in the state before and during the Civil War, the Winslow House attracted great numbers of guests escaping summer pestilences in cities on the Ohio and lower Mississippi Rivers.

claimed the healthfulness of Minnesota's climate to be its "crowning attraction." Never mind its fertile soils, ten thousand lakes, or pivotal location as an entrepôt to westward expansion. "Here, under the influence of bright skies and pure air, the spirits riot in happy consciousness of fresh health and energy, and the ordinary burdens of labor and thought become luxuries." Commissioner H. C. Rogers, like many writers to follow, particularly attended to the state's benefits for sufferers from tuberculosis. "It is indeed," he crowed, "the sanatorium for consumptives."[7]

Hardly had Rogers's tract gotten into circulation when Girart Hewitt, a lawyer, land dealer, and booster *extraordinaire*, privately published a pamphlet on

Minnesota's climate that culminated in a thirty-four-page section on "Minnesota as a Resort for Invalids." Attributed to Dr. Thaddeus Williams, the appendix alternately waxed scientific and ridiculous. A modicum of scientific respectability was maintained by such features as a table from the 1860 U. S. census showing that Minnesota's mortality rate was second only to Oregon's. But on the whole Williams's statement was little more than a flurry of breathtaking claims and colorful anecdotes. In Minnesota, he reported, the air was so free of moisture for most of the year that "meat hung up dries before it spoils." Furthermore, people who "have had but one lung for ten years" reached such a state of health that no one knew them to have had tuberculosis. To his credit, however, Dr. Williams stopped short of picking up the putrid tale that quickly became a mainstay of Minnesota's sanatorial promotions in the aftermath of the Civil War. First written down by Hartford, Connecticut, physician Horace Bushnell, its leading character was a man who coughed up bits of his lung the size of a walnut. After seven months of Minnesota weather, he was sound as a bell.[8]

In the 1870s and 1880s, the tabloid tone of Minnesota health promotions gradually gave way to high-sounding phrases with scientific overtones. Ledyard Bill, a New York writer of unknown experience in the state, wrote a thick pamphlet of thirteen chapters, six of them devoted to Minnesota's climate and its suitability for invalids. His most astonishing claim was that "laboring men in the lumber districts to the north of St. Paul perform their work without overcoats, and frequently, and indeed commonly, without a coat of any kind, simply in their shirtsleeves." This peculiar behavior was explained by reference to that same miraculous dry climate that cured meat on the hook. In Minnesota, "the body maintains a much greater amount of animal heat." To cover his claims with a veneer of scientific respectability, Bill cited statistics derived from the 1870 census showing that the state's mortality rate from consumption was one-fifth that of Massachusetts.[9]

The high point of medical hype occurred in 1885 when a resort community rag known as the *Northwestern Tourist* gathered into a single article the ruminations of half a dozen local authorities. None offered a titillating tale of cure in the manner of their 1860s predecessors, but the prose had it own vaporous charms. "There is," one doctor mused, "a peculiarity in the air. Upon some individuals it has the effect of champagne, each inspiration being a positive enjoyment. This cool, bracing and elastic atmosphere producing increased physical and mental power appears to be the main factor. The nutritive changes, the complete revolution in the interstitial deposit necessary to a cure, I am convinced will not occur in the warm, relaxing climate of Florida." Another doctor coupled climatic with geographic considerations. The location of the state as the "height of land" from which the three great waterways of the continent flowed gave it unusually efficient drainage, and even its morasses were harmless because it was "late in the spring before they became heated sufficiently to generate miasm." The ranking physician of the group, president of the state board of health D. W. Hand, even claimed a comparative exemption of the state's residents from catching colds.[10]

Chroniclers of Minnesota's past echoed the increasingly mysterious, pseudo-scientific language of the state's propagandists. By the time Henry Castle wrote his three-volume history of the state in 1915, advertising Minnesota's cold winters had lost all pretense of scientific reasoning and become an exercise in verbal euphorics. The winter air of Minnesota, claimed Castle, was "a germicide of unquestioned potency, a microbe quencher of purest ray serene"; its winter climate caused men to "overspill vigor and virility."

With phrases such as these on the page, Castle's specification of nine virtues of the Minnesota winter seemed a pedantic redundancy.[11]

Until the population explosion of the Twin Cities in the mid-1880s, the more spiritual benefits to be derived from an active embrace of Minnesota winters seldom found their way into print. Goodhue was not alone, however, in insisting on the supraphysical virtues of wintry activities. On the aesthetic side, as early as 1852 a Minnesota traveler named John P. Owens ridiculed the very idea of winter travel in a closed carriage. "What is sleigh-riding worth, if you are enclosed as in a jail, and can see nothing of the beauties of the winter scenery as you pass along? Of all the abominations we ever knew in traveling, save us from a covered sleigh." Of course, the traveler who wanted to enjoy the open air had to make certain adjustments. Owens recommended dispensing with the usual hat, cloak, gloves, and boots in favor of a cap "to come well over the ears," a thick overcoat piled on top of woolen drawers and leggings, fur mittens, and two pairs of woolen socks followed by buckskin moccasins and buffalo overshoes. Once these small adjustments were made, anyone "who desires to visit Minnesota in the winter season, and is deterred for fear of difficulties or sufferings on the road is either a dunce or is very chicken-hearted, and would never amount to a great deal after he got here."[12]

The "never amounting to a great deal" resonates with the second of Goodhue's themes — that winter energizes as it uplifts. The same amateur essayist who introduced Minnesotans to Dr. Bushnell's tale about lungs and walnuts characterized the Minnesota winter as "a season of ceaseless business activity and constant social enjoyment."[13] This theme rose to special prominence in the 1880s, when the bane of winter was often held to be not cold but a prolonged thaw. A corpulent visitor grumbled to a local reporter that he was "too fat to enjoy" the warm weather and that "this is about the first time I ever suffered through a December in a Northern city."[14] While St. Paul's third winter carnival was underway, the *Northwestern*

Northern Pacific Sanatorium in Brainerd, ca. 1904

Magazine devoted an article to Minnesota winters, averring that "comfortable" winter weather in St. Paul ranged from ten below at daybreak to ten above during the height of the sun. At those temperatures, "the air is clear and wonderfully invigorating and the sun shines brightly," leading to universal good spirits and business going on "with a vim." Most importantly, "you are surprised at the amount of work you can do in a day without fatigue. You feel like a well-groomed race horse. And then how soundly you sleep and what an appetite you have!"[15]

For all of the hyperbole about winter's physical, intellectual, and spiritual benefits, there would have been little incentive actually to time festivals and other celebrations to its harsh conditions without the third theme — that cold could be fun. Naturally, it was not the cold itself but things that could be done only if it were prolonged and deep. The theme of winter as fun developed side by side with the emergence of recreational activities and entertainments specifically adapted to icy or snowy conditions. Pioneering phases of these sports made up the last background condition for the emergence of winter festivals.

INAUGURATING THE CARNIVAL SEASON

"Perhaps the people down in the states," wrote a St. Paul newspaperman in 1849, "imagine that we of Minnesota go into a state of torpidity during our long and severe winters, like the frogs and snakes of their own swamps and marshes." Nothing, he assured his readers, could be further from the truth. Not only do Minnesotans rise at dawn to go about their business, they take in as much winter weather as they can for their enjoyment as well as their health.[2]

What particularly caught the journalist's attention was the custom of reserving winter afternoons and evenings for sleigh rides, either on the Mississippi River or on the crude roads about the city. Even at this early date, the cutters and sleighs of St. Paul's finest could, in his words, "hold their own in Broadway or Tremont Street." Sleighing provided early settlers with a linkage to their New England roots — as well as proof to the doubters back east that Minnesota cold did not preclude simple pleasures. The very stability of the winter freeze assured regular sleighing. As a later commentator observed, "all vehicles go on runners from December until the first of April and the streets and

[facing page]
Tintype of two bustle-challenged young ice skaters of St. Paul in the late 1870s

roads are musical with sleigh bells." Even the most mundane of conveyances had its wheels laid aside, as "cabs, stages, omnibuses and buggies are fitted each with four little steel-shod sleds."[3]

From territorial days, sleigh riding offered the mix of aristocratic preening and low-brow ribaldry that would become characteristic of St. Paul's winter carnivals. Marion Ramsey Furness, the daughter of Minnesota's first territorial governor, recollected St. Paul's "great reputation for fine turnouts, and the high-stepping horses with stylish barouches in summer and in winter the truly regal sleighs decked out with robes — the very finest this fur-bearing country could produce — and tinkling sleigh bells, all combined to make as gay a picture as one could wish to see." Our St. Paul newspaperman, in the meantime, chronicled horses blowing icicles from their nostrils, ladies alter-

nately laughing and screaming, and young men "driving like Jehu, and as full of life and mischief as monkies under a tropical sun." In 1856, a newspaper editor in St. Peter gently chided local boys for driving so recklessly that a sleigh was overturned and a snow bath given "free of charge."[4]

Early sleigh owners, particularly those who had brought their cutters from New England, would not have countenanced risking loss of so expensive and prestige-laden a conveyance by driving it to its limit. Yet sleigh races undoubtedly occurred on an informal basis; too many reins were too often placed in the hands of boys for it to have been otherwise. But pitting sleighs against each other in an organized competition, sanctioned by adults and run with official starting times, a cleared course, and a large audience, awaited the first St. Paul winter carnival.

Five gentlemen out for a sleigh ride down Main Street in Faribault, ca. 1870

Long before the first sleighs arrived in Minnesota Territory, another class of sliding vehicles considerably humbler in construction and societal associations migrated westward with the French voyageurs. These "trains" (a shortening of the French word *traîneau* for sledge) were of two types. In the first, a large wooden box was mounted on runners made of two-inch planks and pulled by a single horse. This was the dominant winter conveyance for Minnesota territorial pioneers and their provisions, and in rural areas it persisted well into the twentieth century. Apart from its use for rural sleigh rides, it was ill adapted for any sport, either in competition or as exhibition. It was the smaller model, pulled by dogs, that had recreational potential. The dog train consisted of little more than a wide board turned up at the forward end. Typically, three dogs pulled it in tandem, and two men controlled its direction and speed, one walking before it and the other behind it.[5]

With the advent of railroads, the dog train all but disappeared from North America. Sustained mainly by French Canadian hunters, trappers, and mail deliverers, it persevered in Minnesota only where the railroad did not yet run. One railroad zealot even attempted to put steam locomotives into service on the Mississippi River between Galena and St. Paul. Though the effort was not intended as a winter amusement, reading the advertisement was certainly sport enough:

> *LOCOMOTIVE ICE TRAINS prepared expressly for travelers on the ice of the Mississippi, with ten cars on each train besides the engine and tender cars, with ample arrangements for meals and for sleeping, being now in readiness, will commence running as soon as the ice is sufficiently strong.*
>
> *PASSENGER CARS will be attached to the train in the rear of the baggage cars, so that passengers may incur as little risk as possible. The trains will stop at all the usual steamboat landings. As this novel enterprise is attended with great expense, it is to be hoped that the public will extend to it their liberal patronage.*

The sporting potential of animal-powered snow trains lay dormant until the inception of dog-sled races in the early years of the twentieth century. Unhitching the dogs from the sledge, however, created a new range of possibilities altogether. The bowed front end, a necessity for planing over deep snow, was ideally suited to downhill coasting. In fact, only by pulling on a rope attached to the rear of the sled was it kept from overrunning the dogs on a steep incline. If the dogs were released altogether, the cargo replaced with human riders, and the vehicle aimed down a slope, the result would be tobogganing.

The word toboggan comes from an Algonquin term devoid of any connotations about its use for play. Invented by northern Indians to transport game or supplies through deep snow, it was constructed of long pieces of poplar or alder lath split to a thickness

Stereopticon view of a mail train on the Lake Superior line, ca. 1870

of one-eighth inch and bound with leather thongs. Either a pair of dogs in tandem or the hunter or his wife would pull it.[6]

However practical its origins, the Indians turned the toboggan to sporting use long before it became a popular pastime among white settlers. The first mention of snow coasting in a Minnesota newspaper

reported several Ojibway sliding downhill near Le Sueur while "standing upon a bit of board" late in the winter of 1850. What made the event newsworthy was not the practice itself, which was already known to be their common method of coasting, but the accident that ensued. One of the Ojibway fell and struck his head, lapsed into a "lethargy," and died.[7]

Between this occurrence and the tobogganing craze that engulfed eastern Canada and spread into the United States in the mid-1880s, little coasting of any sort was deemed worthy of public notice. For most Minnesotans, it remained a childhood diversion, undertaken on a simple, unsteerable sled with wood runners, the rider lying belly down. The juvenile activity came to public attention only if it caused an accident or became a nuisance. In the week before Christmas 1885, Dayton's Bluff on the east side of

St. Paul became so perilous for pedestrians that coasting was outlawed. To bring home the dangers of the sport in the Christmas season, the *Pioneer Press* published a maudlin story about an Italian immigrant whose skillfully wrought carvings were ruined by collision with a boy on a hand sled. "The small boy went back up the hill, while Piettro buried his dream and beloved images in a snowdrift and let fall over them a scalding tear."[8]

Until preparations for St. Paul's first winter carnival began late in 1885, toboggans received even less notice than sleds. One of the earliest Twin Cities reports of their recreational use by whites noted the formation of a tobogganing club in the winter of 1884-85 in Florence, probably meaning a northern Wisconsin community near Iron Mountain. A three-hundred-foot slide was reputed to have taken four seconds to travel, which would come to fifty-one miles per hour. News of the Florence slide apparently failed to reach eastern ears, for the only pre-1886 toboggan slides known to that bellweather of popular recreational tastes, *Frank Leslie's Illustrated Newspaper*, were in Saratoga, New York, and an unidentified town in Vermont.[9]

The ease of achieving breathtaking speeds soon propelled the sport into other cities and resort communities across Canada and the northern states. One of St. Paul's early toboggan enthusiasts exclaimed that going from a hand sled to a toboggan was like changing from a plug to a runaway horse. Another averred that "the whole physical and mental frame is filled with an utterly novel combination of feelings, chief of which are mortal and hair-straightening terror, and an exhilarating and barbarous delight."[10]

As late as 1887, a newspaper editor in Red Wing noted that Webster had yet to include the word "toboggan" in his dictionary. The great lexicographer was no more than a few years behind, for the word did not pass into common American use until the sport burst across the northern tier of states in 1885 and 1886. As a Minneapolis reporter put it, prior to the first St. Paul winter carnival, not one coaster in a

dozen would have known the difference between a toboggan and a gondola. Its native antecedents in the area utterly forgotten, the founders of the St. Paul winter carnival believed that they were introducing the sport to the state.

When St. Paul's claim to priority was published, a paper skirmish ensued. First, a group of high school boys from the Lake Minnetonka town of Excelsior came forward with proof that they had formed a toboggan club on November 4, 1885, anticipating St. Paul's Wacouta Club by two weeks. Loath to see bragging rights leaving his town, a St. Paul reporter quickly countered with a club supposed to have been formed on St. Anthony Hill west of downtown in 1882. Whatever tobogganing's precise local origins may have been, the first St. Paul winter carnival quickly became the catalyst for its spread throughout the state.[11]

Not everyone favored the sudden rush to the tobogganing slides and slopes. It was the first coasting sport to engage women of otherwise unimpeachably feminine character, and what was worse, these women invariably took their short-lived ride in the clutches

Dr. Louis Benepe and his family on a bobsled in St. Paul, ca. 1885

pleasurable muscular excitement. Especially desirable is this in winter," he intoned. Tobogganing, far from a bane, was a "godsend to the American people. [It] sends a tingle through the entire body. By the time a man has reached the end of the slide and drawn his toboggan back again, he is in a warm and physically hilarious condition. He feels his youth coming back, and is seized with an intense yearning to lift up his voice and make a joyful noise of some sort." Rev. Scudder even found a specifically feminine virtue in the sport, for it "stimulates [women's] vital powers and puts roses on their cheeks without the aid of rouge."[13]

As for the moral vulnerability of young ladies on their way down the slide, male journalists readily took up the theme with sly amusement. Local reportage of the craze among the upper classes at Tuxedo Park, New York, closed with a paragraph headed "why she likes it." A man's arm about the waist of his passenger was a necessity, after all, to hold the proper lady upright, and "when the toboggan begins to slew around and there is some danger of completing the slide in an undignified and distressing attitude," she naturally implores her partner to hold on tighter. He in turn, assuming he is not altogether devoid of wit or a misanthrope, must respond at once by taking away what little breath she may have left in her.[14]

A request from a reader for some guidance in proper tobogganing etiquette led to what is surely one of the finest Minnesota pieces on the sport. After claiming that no formal code of rules had heretofore been published, an editor for the *Minneapolis Tribune* in 1886 produced the following outline:

1. When a gentleman takes a lady down the slide and she, by her swaying from side to side, upsets him in the snow, the practice of picking up the toboggan and thumping her over the head with it is now obsolete in good society.
2. Never stop the toboggan half way down the slide and get out to talk to a friend.
3. After a gentleman has broken his leg or his neck he is expected to make his apologies to his com-

of a man. Conservative prelates such as Montreal's Bishop Fabre denounced the costumes and postures undertaken by women who engaged in such winter sports, and his preachment was circulated to Catholic churches in the northern states.[12]

Protesting clergy were a rarity, however, and local divines were quick to praise the Minnesota virtues of the sport. Ecclesiastical endorsement reached its high point with the first St. Paul winter carnival in 1886. Two days before the formal opening of festivities, the Ko-Ko-Ko Toboggan Club of St. Paul elected the Reverend Clay Macauley as their president. In the following week, the Reverend John L. Scudder of Minneapolis's First Congregational Church delivered a long-anticipated lecture on the theme "Shall We Toboggan?" "I welcome any craze that will drag the people out of their homes, workshops and counting houses into the open air and keep them in a state of

panion and withdraw for the evening. It is regarded as bad form to go on sliding unless particularly requested to do so by the lady.

4. It is customary to commence at the top of the slide and slide downwards. When some are sliding up and some down it creates confusion.

5. After having started a lady down the slide you are expected to go down on the toboggan with her. The style of sliding down behind the toboggan on the stomach and hanging on to the cushion with one hand has gone out of fashion in the most select circles.

6. When steering it is unadvisable to seek to get extra purchase by planting your unemployed foot in the small of the back of the lady in front of you.

7. When you get through with the slide you should leave it where you found it. Others may need it after you have gone.

8. In other respects a gentleman on the slide is simply expected to behave as a gentleman does elsewhere.[15]

Tobogganing simply could not be forced into the current social code. The suddenness of the run, the ease and spontaneity with which partnerships could be formed, and the sheer boisterousness of the sport left the usual considerations of decorum and good taste at the top of the hill. Small wonder at its failure to drag any kind of social code or tradition along with it.

Ice skating, on the other hand, soon to become the most decorous of all winter sports (for a time, anyway), arrived in Minnesota by fits and starts. Like sleighing, it followed the first settlers from New England, who had in turn brought it over from Europe. By 1860 it had become a popular pastime

33

among the youth of St. Anthony and Minneapolis, who regularly used a large area of the Mississippi River between the two settlements. But while a multi-faceted social craze for skating swept the more established — and wealthier — towns to the east, it remained the most informal of diversions among pioneers. Easterners built urban skating ponds and indoor arenas, enjoyed rousing displays of fireworks, donned the latest in skating apparel, and glided to the sounds of the town band, while Minneapolitans shoveled the river, built bonfires, dressed in un-adorned layers of wool, and got a few friends to toot some waltzes.

One of the state's early pleasure skaters, Frank O'Brien, described the two types of skates available in the 1860s as "stub-toes" and "turnovers." The former were little more than sole-shaped wooden planks with a flat piece of steel inserted into a groove beneath, the contraption secured to the foot with tarred rope. What O'Brien called turnovers were probably patent-ed models that fastened the blade onto the sole with plates, as in modern skates, and had leather straps for mounting the shoe onto the skate. Neither was very comfortable, neither protected against the cold, and neither supported the ankle in any way. Even "fancy skating" was often accounted a boy's sport because of the strength required.[16]

The arrival of roller skating in the early 1880s dealt a crushing blow to ice skating as a social activity. Indoor skating arenas went up in towns and cities throughout the state, and crowds flocked to see their local favorites compete against skaters of national rep-utation. The putrid air, slovenly decor, and increasing-ly unsavory reputation of these indoor rinks, even in coliseum-like structures such as those built in the Twin Cities, soon stalled the craze, but the damage to cold-weather skating had been done. Fancy and speed skating exhibitions no longer drew audiences, and by 1885 even a downtown St. Paul race pitting United States distance champion James Lilly against famed Canadian skater Charles Lecocq got only the briefest of notices in the local press.[17]

In many communities, only the boundless winter energy of school children and young adults kept ice skating alive. While the sport was in eclipse, the *Pioneer Press* recorded an amusing pairing of youthful skating with a more sedate winter activity planned for ther elders. On Christmas Day 1885, Stillwater chil-dren congregated to skate on a cleared area of Lake St. Croix, while the men of the town gathered for a turkey shoot across the lake. The hunters had the option of firing at the heads of the turkeys at sixty-six yards or at the whole body at two hundred yards.[18]

Like skating, skiing boasted a European pedigree, but it arrived in Minnesota without being filtered through New England. Its initial practitioners in the state were Norwegian settlers who had brought their skis with them. In the 1860s, Pope County in the western part of the state boasted over a dozen immi-grants who regularly used skis as their primary means of winter travel. Many traversed the neighboring county to reach St. Cloud for provisions, a distance of sixty miles as the crow flies. One early settler remembered an 1868 winter encounter with Knut Simon on the road between Sauk Centre and Glen-wood, both on skis and Simon with a hundred-pound sack of flour on his back and a bundle of groceries under one arm.[19]

For these Norwegian pioneers, skiing was a practi-cal necessity. More often than not they strapped the boards on with little thought of having fun. However, the sporting instinct invariably asserted itself in those with an athletic gift. Halvor Jorgenson Hjelstad, known as the most graceful skier among the Pope County Norwegians, would "sashay down the slope of the river until he found a narrow place, then he would retrace his ski marks and get a good start down the slope and jump across the narrowest place in the stream."[20]

Hjelstad's playful jumping in 1868 anticipated by fifteen years the first public demonstration of the sport in Minnesota. Immigrants to America had to await Norway's own discovery of the activity's mass enter-tainment potential. During the 1870s jumping with skis gradually evolved into a national sport in the Old Country. In the long winter evenings, rural youth impressed the ladies in attendance with skiing tricks, while by day the public at large so took to the sport that its champions were royally decorated. Norwegian immigrants from the 1880s on carried the fad with them, and Minnesota was one of their prime destinations.

Largely through the efforts of a single individual, Minneapolis rather than Glenwood became the first city in the nation to boast a skiing association. Carl Ilstrup arrived in 1881, finding work in the city engineering office in the following year. He immediately established the Minneapolis Ski Club and set about enlisting his fellow Norwegians. Favorite skiing spots in those days were on Lowry Hill and Washburn Heights, which at that time offered uninterrupted terrains of nearly treeless slopes.[21]

In 1885 the Minneapolis Ski Club sponsored what was arguably the first ski tournament (then called a ski run) in the United States. Ishpeming, Michigan, a center of American skiing for many years, generally claims that distinction for its own Norwegian ski club, but the first meet in Ishpeming did not take place until February 1888. Minneapolis's prior claim rests on a primitive run organized by Illstrup and his friends on February 23, 1885, held not on the club's familiar sites but on a hill above the Minneapolis and St. Louis Railroad shops. Twenty men from the club participated, and all the prizes were carried off by Mikkel Hemmestvedt, a recent arrival from Telemark whose fame as a skier had preceded him. Hemmestvedt's jump of ninety feet was deemed a magnificent accomplishment, and indeed it compared quite favorably with the longest Norwegian jumps of the period.[22]

Mikkel Hemmestvedt ski jumping at Ishpeming, Michigan, in 1891

To add a cachet of class to his new club and their activity, Illstrup and his fellow Norwegians aggressively promoted the event among the city's wealthy. Their efforts raised enough money for uniforms fashioned of blue woolen lumberjacks' suits with gray trim. Seventy years later an aged Norwegian remembered a crowd of several thousand in attendance, but the event

Minnesota ice fisherman on skis with his shelter on his back, location unknown

received only the slightest of notices in the press. Skis were still so much a curiosity among all but the rural Norwegians that the *Minneapolis Tribune* repeatedly referred to the event as a snowshoe race, even as it described the "exhilarating velocity" with which these "shoes" glided over the jump erected on the hill. The Norwegian champion whom the competition first brought before the public was not even mentioned.[23]

Ski club members on the east side of the city and the entire St. Paul ski club (not yet formally organized, but usually identified in print as the "Norwegian Snow Shoe Club") failed to show up at the competition, leading the Minneapolis skiiers to make several vain attempts to schedule others. Two years of erratic snowfall and dwindling enthusiasm took the club through a sequence of reorganizations. Not even participation in the St. Paul winter carnivals could return the club to its initial vigor. It remained for the farms and small towns where skiing had first entered Minnesota to arouse a more lasting interest in the sport.[24]

To the Aurora Ski Club in Red Wing belongs the honor of truly introducing the pleasures of skiing and ski exhibitions to a major sector of the population. A group of Norwegian Americans in Red Wing concocted the scheme of prevailing upon four of Norway's leading skiers to come to America and settle in their town. All were renowned in their native land, and two of them, the Hemmestvedt brothers, had been decorated by the king.

In later years, the Aurora Club claimed to have held the first American skiing competition in 1884. But no record exists of such a competition other than the 1928 recollections of the club's first president, H. L. Hjermstad. Whatever its proper place in the first American moments of the sport, the Aurora Club soon proved the merit of its founders' Norwegian scheme. Mikkel Hemmestvedt (also spelled Hemmedsvedt and Hemmesvedt), still in his early twenties when he immigrated, dominated the sport in Minnesota for the rest of the decade. In 1886, on the cusp of St. Paul's first winter carnival, the Aurora Ski Club was officially organized, and it went on to become the leading skiing organization in the state. Curiously, of the Norwegian quartet that helped to establish the sport in America, only Hjermstad remained in the city that had sponsored his immigration long enough to join its skiing club.[25]

Curling was another winter sport that took several decades to rise above the status of ethnic curiosity.

Its origins are Scottish, and a Scotsman's game it remained through most of the country until the twentieth century. The first known match on the American continent was played in 1759 by Highlanders under General Wolfe's command on the St. Lawrence River. Lacking the traditional stones, the soldiers settled for cannon balls flattened on one side.

Nearly a century later, in the winter of 1856-57, Scottish immigrants in Blue Earth County, Minnesota, gathered to honor the poet Robert Burns and do a bit of curling on the Maple River not far from Mankato. Taking a page out of Wolfe's book, they used flatirons for stones. These soon gave way to the commoner rural expedient of wooden disks bound with an iron ring, courtesy of the local wheelwright. The Maple River men formally organized as the Blue Earth Valley Burns Club in 1866, but as poetry yielded to sport the name changed to the Maple River Curling Club. In 1880, around the time the name change occurred, the club also began to use the real article, granite stones imported from Scotland.[26]

By 1885 curling clubs had started up in Hastings, Mankato, and Minneapolis, with Anoka and St. Paul soon to follow. In every case, the sporting association grew out of a social club formed by Scottish immigrants or others who could claim Scottish blood; Canada supplied more than a few. Minneapolis's Caledonian Club followed the typical course. Formed in 1884 with a general interest in things Scottish, particularly Burns's poetry, it took only a year for curling to become its chief preoccupation.[27]

One of the many attractions of curling was that it could be played as proficiently by the middle-aged as by the young. Its primary demands were a strong arm, a keen eye, and experience at controlling the direction and speed of the curling stone. Played on a long rectangular course called a rink, the chief objective was to send the stone as close as possible to a small circle at the center of the opposite end, known as the tee. Knocking previously thrown stones in and out of the circles surrounding the tee constituted the game's real challenge. Strategy and technique mystified onlookers, as did the curious practice of influencing the speed of the stone by sweeping the ice in front of it with a broom. Yet, in the aftermath of the winter carnivals of the 1880s, curling became one of the state's most popular winter competitions, a position it retained for two generations.

The last, and certainly least dignified, component of Minnesota's winter celebrations to be rooted in the nineteenth century is ice fishing. Any mention of it before the modern era is problematic, for that nineteenth-century soul was rare indeed who thought its wintry trappings to be anything other than an inconvenience, let alone a cause for celebration. The winter fisherman was just a fisherman who refused to give up when the water got hard. And yet there is much in the early stories that foreshadows the carnival atmosphere of modern ice-fishing contests and the ultimate incorporation of many of these contests into full-fledged winter festivals.

As early as 1850, winter fishing was popular enough that perch the size of brook trout were reported to be caught "in great abundance through holes in the ice, in most of our lakes, with small hooks bated." The call of the ice also served as an excuse to draw men out of the house when company got too close. During Winona's first big Christmas party, a man disappeared from the table and reappeared some time later with a catch of fish. He had found an air hole in the ice on the lake and "had but to dip into the water to get all the fish he wanted." The fruits of his brief escape were welcome additions to the all-too-familiar 1852 fare of corn and venison. Catharine Goddard, hostess of the party, claimed this was the beginning of many winter fishing trips to the lake.[28]

The very ease with which large fish could be caught beneath the winter ice almost extinguished the practice before it had a chance to catch fire as a sport. After watching the size of prize fish fall steadily through the course of several summers, a group of Lake Minnetonka's summer cottagers banded together into an association in the early 1880s. Bearing the auspicious title of Minnesota Fish and Game Protective Association, the group had only one initial purpose: to close down all winter fishing of "their" lake. As members of the association were for the most part Minneapolis residents of significant means and influence, they had little difficulty in pressuring the state government into passing the requisite legislation. On February 24, 1885, a state law went into effect banning all fishing on the lake between November 1 and May 1. As fish houses on the lake were regarded under the law as prima facie evidence of violation, the ban extended to them as well.

Local year-round residents were naturally up in arms over a regulation proscribing all ice fishing regardless of type. Formal opposition to the law immediately arose, based on the theory that thinning out the most easily caught winter species, such as pickerel, would benefit those that were more highly prized, such as black bass. While a handful of legal minds went after the law directly, most of the lake's residents contented themselves with simply flaunting

it. A year after the law went into effect, the upper lake was dotted with fish houses, and farmers in one bay were said to back their wagons onto the lake to retrieve their catch.[29]

The arrest of two violators only further polarized the year-rounders and the vacationers. A crowd collected around the sleigh in which the prisoners, a deputy sheriff, and the detective who had made the complaint waited for the train to Minneapolis. Boys and young men vied in the effort to terrorize the informant, and the deputy joined in with "Give him hell, boys!" A pole was produced to ride the detective on and a halter strap yanked from the sleigh for making a noose, until a local doctor finally stepped in to stop the fun.

More finely tuned fish and game protection legislation would soon remove the blanket proscription of winter fishing. But for the rest of the century that little incident on the shore of Lake Minnetonka would be the closest ice fishing came to being a sport in Minnesota.

FROM SHRINES TO FROLICS

SOCIETY OVERFLOWS ITS BOUNDS

In the building of St. Paul's first great ice castle, all the strands of Minnesota's arctic reputation merged and ascended in a single crystalline monument. Blocks of ice twenty inches thick testified readily enough to the seasonal glaciation of the state; their gathering and fusion into a palatial structure over the course of three weeks proved how well the human mind and body could function in this American Siberia; and the thousands of men, women, and children who swarmed and sported and paraded about the castle grounds bore witness to the fun such frigid efforts could bring about.

St. Paul may have introduced the ice castle and the winter carnival to the United States, but neither idea began here. Their local boosters were quick to credit Montreal, which had centered festivals around an ice palace every winter since 1883. From Montreal, in turn, came tales of romantic Russian origins. Empress Anna constructed a winter palace of ice on the Neva River in the winter of 1739-40, and Empress Elizabeth followed with a much larger one in 1754. Early carnival publicity in St. Paul and the official winter carnival brochure made a point of these exotic precedents.[1]

"Society forgets its old restraints. It overflows its bounds. Staid bank presidents are found sitting in their offices in full toboggan uniform. Solemn businessmen leave the counting rooms to take their place on the floats of the Nushkas or the Owls.... As soon as the Palace was built and Carnival was proclaimed the whole city capitulated."

NORTHWEST ILLUSTRATED MONTHLY MAGAZINE, February 1888

[facing page]
Andrew S. Johnson of St. Paul in a homemade blanket suit costume in 1886

As early as 1867, a small-town Minnesota paper picked up an even earlier instance of a Russian ice palace, supposedly built for Peter the Great in 1720. According to legend, a buffoon in Peter the Great's service asked permission to marry a beautiful woman of the court and, when mocked by his master, turned his caustic wit on him. The emperor repaid him with the woman of his desires and an ice palace, complete with furnishings and chandeliers, only to seal him and his bride up in their nuptial chamber. In its *Wilton Weekly News* rendition of 1867, the tale ends with the luminous tomb gradually giving way to sun and soot until even the emperor could no longer bear to look at its congealed and blackened features.[2]

As it happens, the construction technology of that grisly wedding present was identical to that of the later Russian and Canadian ice palaces and all of the St. Paul ice palaces up to the 1980s. Massive blocks of ice were cut out "as if from stone," then laid up and fastened with water in place of mortar. But the despotic purposes of the Russian ice castle schemes, real and legendary, required some adjustment to modern social conditions. Built by imperial whim for courtly entertainment (including the pleasure of torturing those who had fallen from grace), none was a public monument in the modern sense. The tradesmen and peasants who cut and laid up the blocks of ice could only watch from afar as the emperor or empress led processions of sleighs and imperial guardsmen around the finished structure or held feasts within its halls.

In Montreal, and St. Paul to follow, civic leaders emphasized that the castle grounds were a public meeting place, open to all who wished to participate in the carnival. The North American ice palace in effect converted an emblem of wealth at its most arrogant into a shrine of democracy around which rich and poor, farmer and banker, man and woman, black and white could mix in mutual hilarity, celebration, and sportsmanship.[3]

The idea of creating a winter festival in St. Paul, with an ice palace as its signature, flew in the face of Minnesota's official stance in regard to its winters. The state's appointed propagandists had for many years maintained a policy of pretending that Minnesota winters were nothing if not temperate. Pamphlets for eastern and even southern consumption flowed from the office of H. H. Young, the secretary of the State Board of Immigration, each stressing not only the healthfulness of the Minnesota climate but its superior comfort level to the clammy forty-degree conditions prevailing in, say, New York, Ohio, and Kentucky. In order to impress skeptics with the mildness of Minnesota winters, state promoters led by Girart Hewitt (that same booster who spread the news that meat in Minnesota dried before spoiling) organized steamboat excursions as late in December as the river would permit and posed for correspondents in linen dusters and straw hats.[4]

The early 1880s threw all such pretense into a cocked hat. Three straight winters (1882–83 through 1884–85) recorded mean temperatures in the single digits, a run without precedent since thermometer readings had first been tabulated in the early days of Minnesota Territory. The most dismal piece of Minnesota's winter mythology thus appeared about to crystalize into hard fact, just as the Twin Cities were poised on the cusp of their greatest population boom. Eastern correspondents were merciless in their reports, a New York newspaperman going so far as to announce that St. Paul was "another Siberia, unfit for human habitation in winter."

George Thompson, father of the St. Paul Winter Carnival

That single remark is frequently cited as the impetus for the organization of St. Paul's first winter carnivals. In reality, the hyperbole of eastern journalists was little more than a catalyst in a process that had causes much closer to home. Two events in late 1885 impelled St. Paul business leaders toward the winter carnival idea. First, a smallpox epidemic swept Montreal, quarantining much of the city and ruining hopes for repeating its great attraction of previous winters. George Thompson, editor of the *St. Paul Dispatch*, saw in that misfortune an opportunity for his city to step forward as inheritor of the ice palace legacy.[5]

Of equal importance to Montreal's misfortune was the increasingly heated rivalry between the Twin Cities. After losing a bitter battle over the location of the state fair grounds, Minneapolis boosters raised a subscription in 1885 for an industrial exposition that threatened to dwarf the state fair as a showplace of Minnesota's commercial prowess. Although officially supporting the state fair in St. Paul, some of the exposition's most vocal proponents saw the pending project as a sign of Minneapolis's ascendance. "St. Paul was a sternwheel town," crowed one of them, "and when the sternwheel steamer could pass the locomotive then St. Paul would catch up with Minneapolis."[6]

Thompson saw it as his civic duty to take up the cudgels on behalf of the older city. "St. Paul needs to arouse herself and gird on her armor for the battle of progress," he editorialized. A winter carnival afforded the perfect opportunity. On October 21, he urged the organization of a St. Paul winter carnival before a city in New England seized the initiative, on October 22, he declared "Minneapolis is to have her exposition, St. Paul must have her Ice Palace and winter carnival," and on October 26, he elicited the *Chicago Herald*'s approval of the idea. As that newspaper put it, "Why shouldn't St. Paul have an ice carnival? It is a handsome city, well worth seeing at any time, and in winter it enjoys a steady cold which will be sure to preserve everything in the way of ice palaces which may be constructed."[7]

As an influential member of the chamber of commerce, Thompson was well placed to gather the support of his city's leading businessmen. An ice palace committee with him at the head formally endorsed the idea on October 31, and two days later, on November 2, 1885, the St. Paul Ice Palace and Winter Carnival Association was officially organized. Social favorite and avid sportsman (not to mention merchant prince) George R. Finch was elected president and George Thompson first vice-president.

Two weeks later the association officially incorporated with a thirty-year charter and capital stock limited to fifteen thousand dollars. The recently completed Ryan Hotel, St. Paul's finest hostelry, was

George Finch, president of the 1885–86 St. Paul Ice Castle and Winter Carnival Association in its inaugural year, wore the badges of twenty-four winter clubs on his manly breast when he appeared in the uniform of his company, Auerbach, Finch, and Van Slyke

declared the official headquarters, and the officers set about the task of selling ten-dollar shares of stock. At the end of the first month, news of the association and even a rough description of the ice castle found their way via the *Boston Transcript* into the prestigious *American Architect*. By that time, fifty men had each purchased a two-hundred-dollar block of stock, more than enough to build the castle.[8]

Minneapolis leaders initially balked at St. Paul's brazen effort to carnivalize the cold. Minneapolitans had, after all, hatched their own carnival in the previous winter, a pageant of "unrivaled splendor" with grand processions, scores of dramatic tableaux, and scenery "remarkable for its animation and beauty." But they had also been sensible enough to hold it inside. The Minneapolis papers were loath to admit that local winters were long and cold enough to permit construction of so stark a symbol of glacial triumph as an ice palace. An editor of the *Minneapolis Tribune* used an unusually balmy month of December to criticize her sister city's papers for promoting the misconception that this was a place "where ice palaces bloomed all winter." After correcting this impression by burbling about the crisp, pure air, gleaming sunshine, and soft moonlight of winter in Minnesota (choosing a recent thermometer reading of forty degrees as his paradigm), the writer generously offered the only solution that would both salvage Minnesota's reputation and allow the winter carnival to proceed under such temperate conditions. St. Paul had to import an ice-producing machine.[9]

Newspapermen on the other side of the river laughed at all of this cowering make-believe. On December 29, one St. Paul wag suggested reviving Colonel Hewitt's publicity stunt and holding a steamboat excursion climaxed by a picnic. Two days later, with the ground bare of snow and the temperature still above freezing, the secretary of the winter carnival association, A. S. Tallmadge, walked about town in blizzard wrap. Asked whether he was cold, he retorted "Oh no, I am just getting ready for the cold weather we will have within the next few weeks."[10]

When the onslaught finally came in the first week of January, it was all the carnival propagandists could have hoped for. A statewide blizzard plunged temperatures to twenty degrees below zero, and the editor of the *Pioneer Press* ate his Minneapolis peers and the board of immigration for breakfast. In a "new view of the ice palace," he declared

The building of an ice palace in St. Paul, where, thanks to Mr. Young's able pamphlets, the well instructed immigrant would expect to find wild roses and violets blooming in January, will have a disastrous effect in undoing [his] salutary work. The opinion that once prevailed that the winter climate of Minnesota is cold, and which it has cost so many thousands of dollars to dissipate, is likely to become generally current once more. . . . We can only think of one way to counteract the mischievous impression that our Minnesota winter temperature ever reaches the freezing point, and that is for the board of immigration to authorize its able secretary to issue a circular for general distribution throughout Europe and America, explaining that the ice palace is constructed of artificial ice such as is now produced by well understood chemical processes in all hot climates. . . . Meanwhile the newspapers we are sure can be depended upon to second the zealous efforts of Mr. Young . . . by carefully insisting that the toboggans run on rollers, that the suits worn by the toboggan clubs are made of cotton sheeting, and that the snow shoe clubs are picked organizations of young men and maidens, formed to gather flowers.[11]

St. Paul, in fact, had a better idea than this tropical puffery: openly embrace the most extravagantly arctic picture that American people have of Minnesota winters, lure even the most arctophobic easterners and southerners into the state capital with a carnival to end all carnivals, and prove to the stoutest skeptics that Minnesota at ten degrees below zero is more comfortable, more healthful, and more enjoyable than their own states in the summer. The winter carnival would thereby "abolish the popular dread of Northwestern frigidity," and St. Paul would stand out as a city that devotes the heart of its winter to pleasure, while attending strictly to the business of advancing its material interests and those of the Northwest for the remaining fifty weeks of the year.[12]

One of the first orders of business was to form organizations that would be pivotal to the carnival's success, the snowshoe and toboggan clubs. Thousands of Canadians had been educated to a love of these quintessential cold-weather sports by the Montreal carnival, and St. Paul stood to do the same thing for its citizenry in what Thompson called "the most blessed winter climate that God ever manufactured for his beloved children." Establishing a St. Paul snowshoe club was easily accomplished, for St. George's Snowshoe Club of Montreal had branches throughout eastern Canada and was anxious to gain an American

foothold. Some of its leaders had already contacted the carnival organizers and dangled the lure of their attendance and that of snowshoers all over Canada. Those who wanted to piggyback St. Paul snowshoe clubs onto local summer sports organizations rather than the Montreal club were heard and defeated, though the mercurial rise of the sport ultimately permitted them to get their way as well.[13]

Toboggan clubs were an even easier matter. Putting out the word and building a few slides was enough to spawn the formation of over forty clubs by the time the festival opened. These toboggan associations provided the heart and soul of the 1886 carnival. The first clubs, the Wacouta and the Nushka, were composed of men of high social standing, many of them

A few Nushka Toboggan Club members out on a tramp in front of their Summit Avenue headquarters

The first game played in St. Paul, held on the river on Christmas Day, amused spectators with such outcries as "Soop it up" and "Thank ye, Willie!"[15]

On December 7, the Norwegian Snow Shoe Club (as the newspaper first referred to it) regrouped, elected officers, and exhibited its wares, the four-inch-by-eight-foot wooden slats known by them as skis. Like curling, skiing was still largely regarded as an ethnic oddity. For the duration of the first winter carnival, the St. Paul and Minneapolis press continued to refer to what the Norwegian sportsmen wore on their feet

The Ryan Toboggan Club posing on the 1886 carnival grounds. Headquartered at the Ryan Hotel, this was the most prestigious of the many juvenile clubs formed in the first year of the carnival.

serving on the chamber of commerce or other organizations that were privy to the earliest discussions of carnival plans. But soon enough, business concerns headed by carnival supporters began to sponsor their own tobogganing associations. Manufacturers, jobbers, and retail merchants all jumped on the carnival wagon. Women, who were allowed participation only as honorary members in the first clubs, responded to the stricture by forming their own organizations. School children did the same thing when barred from the exclusive clubs by their age. By carnival time St. Paul could rightly claim to have displaced Saratoga, New York, as the tobogganing capital of the country.[14]

Other sporting clubs soon cropped up as well, galvanized by the coming carnival to speed a process of organization that was already taking place. Local curlers unexpectedly stole a march on both the tobogganers and snowshoers by forming a St. Paul club on November 16, the very day that articles of incorporation had been filed by the carnival association. Still the nearly exclusive domain of Scotsmen, the sport remained a mystery to the public at large.

as a kind of shoe. By an unfortunate coincidence, the Norwegian pronunciation of "ski" approximates "she" in English, which was close enough to the pronunciation of "shoe" to confirm the association. In the meantime, to the irritation of the skiers, such members of the public as had actually seen the word in print pronounced it "sky." Today's English pronunciation was as yet foreign to everybody.[16]

Once local sporting organizations had begun to fall in place, the carnival association turned its attention to the castle. Following the advice of local architect

Charles E. Joy, the directors called in the Hutchinson brothers from Montreal, creators of each of that city's ice palaces. As the senior partner of the firm, Alexander Hutchinson produced the designs, while J. H. Hutchinson assisted in overseeing construction and dealing with clients. Both were Scotsmen with equal enthusiasm for ice sports and glacial architecture.[17]

On December 1, J. H. Hutchinson stepped off the train from Montreal, drawings in hand for the crystalline castle that smallpox had banished from his own city. Most likely these were the plans reported in the *American Architect* the week before. Members of the winter carnival association showed Hutchinson two potential locations: the upper island (known today as Harriet Island) on the Mississippi River and Central Park, an as yet undeveloped tract just north of downtown, at the east edge of the present capitol mall. These locales have remained prime sites for winter carnival activity to the present day.

Hutchinson immediately expressed a preference for Central Park and worked up a site plan, locating the ice castle at the center, children's toboggan slides on the gently sloping roads at either side, a taller main slide down Cedar Street farther to the west, and a quartering of the remaining land into playing fields and ice rinks. After several days of mulling over the castle plans and other arrangements, the association finally tendered the Hutchinson firm a contract, with the stipulation that St. Paul builder James Brodie would act as local contractor. The junior partner returned to Montreal to await the end of Christmas festivities.[18]

Carnival association members expressed only one complaint about the ice palace plan: it lacked the requisite degree of grandeur. This was good news for the architects. St. Paul at last offered them the opportunity to develop the expansive interior spaces and vast, unbroken walls of ice that a cramped site had denied them in Montreal. In the finished scheme, a massive central tower jutted outward in all directions, and the surrounding wall bristled with smaller towers and ramparts; this much expanded on its Montreal predecessors.

But there was a trick behind the scattered disposition of all these picturesque bits of castellated ice. From outside the walls, the castle loomed as a single palatial pile; from inside, the sense of continuous mass and structure dissolved into four open plazas with the tower as a centerpiece. Initial plans to roof the tower and plazas with canvas were abandoned on the basis of Montreal's experience. Direct daylight not only illuminated the activities within but enhanced the brilliance of the surface for those viewing the castle from afar.[19]

No description of the ice palace was complete without an impressive array of statistics particularizing its dimensions and construction. The structure as a whole was 140 by 175 feet, or about twice the size of

Pulling ice blocks from the Mississippi River for use in the ice palace

its largest Montreal predecessor. Its central tower rose one hundred feet on walls four feet thick. Perimeter and connecting walls were made of blocks forty-four inches wide, twenty-two inches deep, and twenty inches high, which was the depth of the ideal ice cut. Twenty thousand blocks of ice weighing five thousand tons required more than one hundred workmen on the site every day for close to two weeks.[20]

When Alexander Hutchinson arrived to oversee construction on December 29, the weather was so balmy that mud appeared to be more readily available than ice as a building material. Even after the blizzard of early January, the architect continued to fret that the ice was not thick enough for good construction. A cold wave on the ninth, sending temperatures to thirty degrees below zero, stilled his complaints. By the twelfth, ice on the clear central channel of the Mississippi had reached the depth of fifteen inches, and by the seventeenth it had achieved the ideal thickness of twenty inches.[21]

As cartloads of ice rolled up the streets and the castle began its glittering ascent, St. Paul residents could scarcely stay away from the grounds. "It is carnival on the streets, carnival at the hotels, carnival at home, carnival everywhere," announced the *Pioneer Press*. A month later *Harper's Weekly* echoed the theme. "The whole city has given itself up, heart and pocket and hand, to the spirit of the carnival."[22]

The sudden arrival of the weather for which Minnesota was famous squelched the castle's last vocal critics, and cities from Minnesota to Montana began to vie for contributions to the structure. Stillwater sent a cornerstone block eight feet square and twenty inches thick, only to be informed that the association had already accepted an offer from Fargo, Dakota Territory; both blocks were worked into the cornerstone-laying ceremony. Ortonville, on the Dakota Territory boundary, wanted to ship a block of ice thirty feet long, ten feet wide, and thirty inches thick; Glenwood, also in western Minnesota, sent a block six by three by three feet; the Dakota towns of Wahpeton and Watertown forwarded blocks six by five by two feet and six by four by three feet, respectively; and Devil's Lake, Dakota Territory, donated a monumental block for the arch to the main entrance. Not to be outdone by such distant outposts, the nearby resort lakes of White Bear and Minnetonka contributed enough loads of ice to construct the north and south bastions of the palace.[23]

With the building of the castle underway, firm carnival dates were finally set for the first two weeks of February. But the fun began well in advance of the official opening. Toboggan club members endlessly

"tested" the new slide while it was under construction, and other slides began to pop up around the city. Snowshoe clubs held tramps up Summit Avenue, and St. George's Snowshoe Club introduced "bouncing" as an initiation exercise for new members and a way of forcing the stuffiest of public figures into the circle of fun. Supposedly of Cossack Russian origin, it consisted of tossing the honored individual as high in the air as possible, then catching him with outstretched arms before sending him aloft again. As a frequent witness of bouncings observed, "the only course for the 'bounce' is passive non-resistance, and struggling in the air whilst ascending and descending only adds to the ludicrous appearance of the victim." Local practitioners first bounced with the arms alone, but by carnival time blankets with handles along the edges were in common use.[24]

Numerous clubs formed or sprang into action in the middle of January, spurred by the opportunity to participate in the cornerstone-laying ceremony. The

49

Norwegian skiing club was out and about and encouraging the Minneapolis club to join them. Minneapolis and St. Paul sportsmen also met in the first match between their curling clubs, played in subzero temperatures on January 22. George Thompson spearheaded the organization of the city's first outdoor skating association, appropriately named the Carnival Skating Club. Even a winter hunting association sprang up. Dubbed the Ice Bear Club, its professed purpose was "to hunt rabbits and enjoy life," but its first function was to add the discharge of guns to the din of carnival parades.[25]

Grand processions and parades figured heavily in the carnival spectacle. When carnival organizers decreed that a showy uniform was required for parades and was as good as a ticket for all other carnival events, the clubs made an unprecedented rush on wool blankets, moccasins, and the services of local tailors. Fifty clubs fell into place by the first week in February, most of them decked out in an ensemble of pants and coat, toque (a sort of stocking cap), sash, stockings, and moccasins. St. George's Snowshoe Club, the trend setter for those who could keep up, assembled a costume for $13.50. While assuring its readers that this was a very "serviceable" sort of costume, the *Pioneer Press* offered a cheaper alternative. Two blankets bought at wholesale could make three suits, and mass purchases of the other items as well could keep the total cost between eight and eleven dollars, depending on the quality of the blanket and whether the suit was made at home.

Sales of sporting equipment also boomed. Toboggans from Quebec fetched as much as nine dollars in St. Paul, due largely to duty and shipping costs. By the middle of January, home manufacture was well under way, permitting the purchase of a sound toboggan for as little as two dollars. Ice skates had been gathering dust on local store shelves since the roller skating craze of 1884, an indoor winter entertainment that by then had accumulated enough shoddy social trappings to earn the universal condemnation of the clergy. Carnival enthusiasm returned skaters to the out-of-doors, where the air was too cold for immorality, and wares from the seventy-five-cent blunt-toe to the ten-dollar nickel-soled club skate began to move again.[26]

Festivities officially began two weeks before the opening of the carnival, with the laying of the cornerstones. St. Paul at last had the opportunity to see what the carnival might come to. Electric lights flooded the unfinished ice palace while thousands of people strained for the sounds of band music that would announce the beginning of the procession.

The Great Western Band was honored with the front position, followed by George R. Finch and the "the prettiest young lady that could be found to perform the ceremony of laying the block" together with her escorts. By a not so strange coincidence, the prettiest was Finch's own daughter, Clementine. They were followed by the proper entourage of dignitaries and then — the heart of the occasion — the first massed public appearance of the winter clubs in uniform. St. George's Snowshoe Club, now 125 strong, marched to shouts of admiration mixed with an occasional "Take those bladders off your feet!" Then came the Wacouta tobogganers, the first to organize a club in the city; the Nushkas wearing flaming red outfits and carrying Chinese lanterns; and all the rest. Perhaps the profoundest impression was made by the Ice Bear Club, which fired simultaneous volleys from their shotguns at intervals of five minutes. Horses reared and women screamed.[27]

From Boston came the finest piece of equipage in the carnival, a sleigh in the form of a ship's hull drawn by eight horses and capable of carrying forty people. It was filled by two little boys' toboggan clubs. Another crowd favorite, but for satiric reasons, was an ominously dark sleigh facetiously held to be a Black Maria, bearing dignitaries from the St. Paul Chamber of Commerce. Firemen, postal workers, and military cadres closed out the parade.

Only the Windsor Snowshoe Club allowed its female members to participate in the procession, though many of the other clubs were open to both sexes; indeed several had been formed by girls and women. Leaving women out of the parade conformed to the wishes of the carnival association, but that would soon change. Public response to the appearance of the women snowshoers, tobogganers, and skaters in their blanket suits was so overwhelming that the organizers of ensuing parades were forced to suspend their ideas of decorum. Of all the carnival events, women

would ultimately be excluded only from the storming of the castle, a bit of male foolishness from which many probably were grateful to be delivered.[28]

With the two cornerstones properly anointed with water from a silver pitcher, the speechifying began.

Scenes from the grand parade published in *Frank Leslie's Illustrated Newspaper*

Governor Lucius Hubbard canonized Minnesota winters and alluded to the recent "singular spectacle of the people of this city beseeching for a blizzard as fervently as the victims of a drought-stricken district ever wishes for rain." Mayor Edmund Rice waxed eloquent on the democratic underpinnings and unsurpassed beauty of the spectacle, quoting Keats and scripture to back him up. Minneapolis Mayor George Pillsbury and the Honorable E. W. Durant of Stillwater made similarly profound and happy remarks, and the exercises came to an end.[29]

To ensure that rumors and news correspondents' reports were not all that the nation would hear of the coming festivities, the carnival association organized a massive publicity campaign. Twenty thousand copies of a carnival souvenir pamphlet were distributed through the Twin Cities area, at least three thousand color lithographs of the ice palace found their way into every corner of the nation, and twelve immense gilded and frosted lithographs were shipped or carried to Chicago, St. Louis, New Orleans, and several eastern cities for public exhibition. Carnival association vice-president George Thompson made a grand circle through Milwaukee, Chicago, Kansas City, Atchison, St. Joseph, Council Bluffs, Omaha, and Sioux City, remaining a day in each place to boost the carnival and distribute advertising circulars.[30]

Although skepticism about the carnival's chances for success refused to die out entirely, several midwestern cities provided extensive coverage of St. Paul's plans and preparations. Early in January, the *Chicago Tribune* and *St. Louis Globe Democrat* published feature articles with half-page illustrations of the ice palace. Similar features in *Frank Leslie's Illustrated Newspaper* and *Harper's Weekly* brought highlights and pictures of the carnival to a national audience.[31]

Minneapolis pitched in by dispatching a witty press release to the *Chicago Mail*. Headlined "The Ice Palace at St. Paul Destroyed by the Flames," the article obviously drew its inspiration from the earlier scoffing of Chicago (and Minneapolis) newspaper correspondents at the idea of building an ice palace in a climate as "mild" as their own. Along the way, the writer satirized the fire escape recently invented by a Stillwater judge, the practice among St. Paul's elite of dressing up like Indians, Thomas Lowry's Minneapolis streetcars, and the self-seriousness of some of Minneapolis's leading citizens. After assigning the fiery catastrophe to natural causes (a certain local judge and army veteran having smiled just as the castle was nearing completion), the writer proceeded to a proper description of the ice palace, complete with its Russian and Canadian forebears.[32]

Statewide publicity required a different approach, for carnival organizers wished to engage other Minnesota communities in the festival as active participants. The "storming" of Stillwater, Hastings, and Red Wing by uniformed clubs aroused enough interest for each community to create its own toboggan clubs and assure the participation of Red Wing's Aurora Ski Club. Stillwater's toboggan club immediately set about

constructing its own slide, a seven-hundred-foot chute running through a ravine in the hill south of downtown. The town was known for its penal institution and its lumbering business, creating two distinct possibilities for thematic costumes. Carnival organizers plumped for a column of marchers robed in the black-and-white stripes of traditional prison garb, but the Stillwater club chose the more decorous option, Mackinaw plaid lumbermen's outfits. These were converted to costumes by shortening the pants into knee breeches, showing the marchers' long, bright red stockings to maximum effect.[33]

Word of interest in the carnival from Litchfield, Mankato, and Faribault opened them up to a raid as well, but frigid weather and the resulting halt in railroad traffic foiled tentative plans for excursions. The citizens of Faribault were so incensed by their perceived slight that the St. Paul clubs decided to make up for lost time by splitting up into three parties and raiding the towns simultaneously on January 27, five days before the festival. Each raid bore its own particular charms: the Mankato excursion for the unusual predominance of ladies, the Faribault trip for streets so deep with snow that the parade stalled, and the Litchfield visit for the repeated failures of the Litchfield Bouncing Club to fulfill its mission safely and properly.[34]

George Finch had statewide business contacts and did not hesitate to use them as a means of extending invitations to other towns. In the middle of January, Brainerd tobogganists organized the Pine Tree Club, Northfield formed the Acme Toboggan Club, Norwegians in Zumbrota created the Viking Ski Club, and Duluth established a snowshoe and toboggan association. For some time Duluthians had known their city to be all too well suited for winter sports. Two weeks before receiving word of Finch's invitation, a local paper chided the city authorities about a street that "would be a treasure to the St. Paul Ice Carnival Association if it could only be borrowed for a toboggan slide." Said to be composed entirely of "explorers and snowshoeists," the Duluth club promptly made plans for a slide on the bay of Lake Superior, ordered uniforms, and began to bargain with the railroads for reduced rates to St. Paul.[35]

Publicity at home required very little effort on the part of the carnival association. Newspapermen usually starved for local January stories wrote daily accounts of club activities, ice palace progress, the planning of the carnival, and the growing adornment of the city. Dressing up the streets and buildings became an effective means of publicity in itself by creating an atmosphere of expectation and showing to all that the festival was to be a citywide affair.

The Hutchinsons' contractual responsibilities ended with the palace and palace grounds; for the rest, the city was left to its own devices. From December to the second week of February, downtown streets and squares gradually displayed the efforts of local sculptors and architects as well as the enterprising businessmen themselves. The first sculptural pieces to be completed were short-lived. An ice statue representing a draped female figure with her hand on an anchor stood in front of carnival headquarters at the Ryan Hotel just before Christmas. Shortly after its appearance, a "little man with a full black beard" circulated through the crowd claiming the work as his own and announcing that it was but a taste of what awaited them at the carnival. A brief taste it was, for warm weather made slush of it before the first block of the ice palace was set. When the January blizzard initiated castle construction, that same black-bearded sculptor, now identified as O. F. Lewis, carved another advertisement, this time transforming a block of ice into a model of the castle. The Ryan Hotel site was unkind to this as well, and it had to be replaced by a castle made of confectionery and encased in glass, presumably to keep eager fingers away.[36]

Undaunted by the short life of his first efforts, Lewis promptly set to work on a larger model with a three-foot tower, this time detailing all of the turrets and cutting through the window openings. Its immediate future secured by a temperature of twenty below zero, Lewis's second model went on display in front of

a store on West Tenth Street. Many other sculptures soon complemented his effort. The people of White Bear Lake promised a twelve-foot polar bear but came through with a three-foot figure accompanied by a cub, the whole described as "a symphony in milk." This appears to have been a voluntary rather than a commissioned effort. Lewis himself, in partnership with a man named Flint, contributed figures of a Greek slave, a standing woman, and a fierce fight between Samson and the lion, all installed on the palace grounds. Each likely to have been derived from popular paintings, their scantily dressed subjects must have created a bizarre counterpoint with the materials out of which they were made. At least one monumental ice sculpture was commissioned by the association itself: a carving of an Indian spearing a buffalo, scaled at one and a half times life size and placed on a high pedestal at Bridge Square on the southern edge of downtown.[37]

Architect Charles A. Wallingford took charge of building numerous arches over city streets as well as the pedestal for the Bridge Square sculpture. Gabled arches sheathed in ice-clad evergreens spanned each entry to the intersections at Third and Cedar, Fourth and Sibley, and Seventh and Minnesota. Their framework was gas piping, perforated for the installation of burners and colored globes. Ice sculptures on the piers supporting the arches gave each of the intersections a distinctive theme. The first had figures of a

Ice sculpture of Indian hunter and bison at Bridge Square

trapper, an Indian, a bear, and a deer; in the last, a snowshoer stood guard at each corner, while the arches themselves were shaped to resemble the gables of a Swiss cottage. Over the Minnesota Street entry to the carnival grounds, the fourth and grandest of all the arches embraced the pedestrian walks as well as the carriage drive with a tripartite span.[38]

At least one residential neighborhood created its own carnival monument. On January 30, the day before the carnival officially opened, a crystal tower rose in Kelly's Park on Dayton's Bluff. Initially intended to reach the ice palace height of one hundred feet, it stopped at seventy-five. Electric illumination, nightly fireworks, and the proximity of a mammoth toboggan slide and skating rink, also built by neighborhood residents, turned it into an East Side outpost of the carnival.

Young ice skaters in their carnival costumes on a rink in Dayton's Bluff

Many of the city's finest residential neighborhoods underwent transformations timed to the opening of the carnival. A city engineer prepared a sleigh-racing track on Summit Avenue by scraping the snow with the aid of a horse team, then inviting the public to

pack the course down by driving over it. Several of the toboggan clubs constructed a half-mile slide below the avenue on Ramsey Hill. Longer and steeper than the carnival run, it proved to be the precursor of many other toboggan slides on the site. The Dayton's Bluff club built a nine-block-long slide on the "Russian plan," with inclines at either end facing each other so that coasters did not have so far to walk to take a second run. At Crocus Hill, three of the city's most prestigious winter sports associations, the Wacouta, Nushka, and Windsor clubs, built a private run over two thousand feet long with a precipitous fall of ninety feet in the initial two-hundred-foot slide. Like the main slide on the carnival grounds, the upper inclines of all of these were flooded with water in the morning to maintain the requisite layer of glare ice. Minneapolis built several toboggan runs of its own, with a St. Anthony slide carrying coasters nearly across the Mississippi River, another on Sixth Avenue North, and two in the increasingly prestigious Lowry Hill neighborhood.[39]

By the time the long-awaited day arrived and the carnival grounds officially opened to the public on January 31, St. Paul had formed fifty-three winter sports clubs with a combined membership of four thousand. Two thousand toboggan club members, to say nothing of the public at large, now faced the prospect of being funneled into the three chutes on the carnival grounds or trudging to the double chutes on Ramsey Hill or Dayton's Bluff. Fortunately, the splendid blanket suits, the camaraderie, and, above all, the parades were as much an attraction for membership as the sport itself.

It was the parades and castle ceremonies, and all the pomp and pyrotechnics that accompanied them, that made a permanent mark on the consciousness of both native and visitor. On February 1, a grand procession with five thousand torch-bearing uniformed members of local and visiting bands and sports clubs followed a course leading through the city's ice-clad arches, between continuous banks of red fires and festively decorated facades, to the brilliantly illuminated walls

The Start.   J. Anderson

The Ramsey Hill toboggan slide, from a drawing by local scenic and architectural artist John Anderson

of the ice castle, all at a temperature of fourteen below zero. Two days later, with the appearance of the mythical King Borealis, chosen members of the clubs were ensconced on elaborate floats. The Windsor Club float, designed by Wallingford and club member C. J. Monfort, was in the form of an enormous blue-and-white toboggan decorated with red lanterns and the Windsor banner and drawn by six horses. Said to be the most artistic feature of the parade, its special lure to public attention was not the float itself but "the beautiful burden it bore": all fifty lady members of the club, enveloped in fleecy white robes.[40]

These were but the first of many elaborate ceremonial occasions, each of the ensuing eight days of the carnival opening with sporting events and climaxing with a parade or castle festivity. On February 5, the assault on the castle by the Fire King provided an excuse to set off an unprecedented fireworks display. Private citizens had been encouraged to purchase all the fireworks they could afford prior to the assault, so that the procession up to the castle would offer a fore-taste of the main event. In the meantime, the pyro-technician in charge vowed to make the ice palace "look like hell," and from all accounts he succeeded. Six days later, on February 11, came Saturnalia. While colored fires illuminated the ice castle, one hundred fire balloons, ranging in diameter from fifteen to twen-ty feet, simultaneously rose from the ground, initiating yet another and grander display of fireworks. At the end of an afternoon given over to children, the final pyrotechnic activity occurred on February 13, with a display of daylight fireworks and animal balloons.[41]

A number of activities derived from summer pas-times accompanied the winter club sports of snow-

The St. Paul Toboggan Club using what appears to be the Crocus Hill toboggan slide, although it was built for the private use of the Wacouta, Nushka, and Windsor clubs

shoeing, tobogganing, skating, skiing, and curling. The snowshoers played baseball and lacrosse, the skaters engaged in an ice polo tournament, and those gentlemen who wished to remain above the general rowdiness of the carnival retreated to the river, where a track was cleared for trotting and pacing races.

Other activities were offered exclusively or primarily as exhibitions. The carnival association purchased two dog trains from Winnipeg, with four teams and four sledges in each. They were joined in the second week by a dog train belonging to a private citizen of St. Paul. Bred by the Hudson Bay Trading Company for mail delivery, this latter train had also seen service with the Canadian Pacific Railroad. All of the dog trains regularly appeared in parades and hung about

the carnival as a sort of historical curiosity. Visitors rode on sleds behind the carnival association teams in much the same spirit as they rode behind sleighs pulled by moose. There was little thought of competitions; the handful of French Canadians who attended the teams were probably regarded with as much curiosity as their animals, and on any account racing was not traditional among them.[42]

One of the most ballyhooed exhibits of the carnival was an encampment of a hundred Indians. The organizers requested them to dress in their garb of twenty years ago and live in traditional tepees. Their exhibition at the carnival was a tragic commentary on both the humiliation of their present condition and the continuing failure of the conquering culture to see them as more than amusing primitives. The sorriest — and most popular — event in which they were involved was a parade. They willingly re-enacted a war march, the men leading with chants and whoops and the women trailing behind, laboring under the burden of their dismembered village. Indians were also pitted against each other in snowshoe races and against professional sprinters in foot races. No public protest at any of the ways they were lodged or used was recorded in the local papers, and the reporters felt free to describe the character and appearance of the "savages" in the most offensive terms.[43]

Rediscovery of the moccasin sounded the one positive note regarding the Indian presence at the winter

festival. A required part of most club uniforms, it was also touted as the most comfortable foot covering in cold weather. Purchasing a pair of high-topped moccasins became as urgent a requirement for getting into the spirit of the carnival as taking a toboggan run. The Indians, in the meantime, whose prior experience with selling their traditional footwear had been akin to begging, suddenly had more business than they could handle.[44]

Apart from reducing the agony of the Indian to amusing tableaux, the first St. Paul Winter Carnival was amazingly free of commercialism. As many as thirty thousand daily visitors to the city created demands for both comestible and dry goods that city

Sleigh riding on the Mississippi River under the High Bridge, from a drawing by John Anderson

1886

merchants were ill equipped to handle, but prices showed no more fluctuation than during normal winters. Carnival organizers despaired of being able to find lodging for the five thousand non-residents requiring it each day, but hotelkeepers maintained their normal rates, and downtown businessmen scrambled to equip unused spaces with cots so that none would have to be lodged elsewhere. Only saloonkeepers appeared overly anxious to cash in on the carnival, and their leasing of land next to the carnival grounds drew considerable local protest. One

erected a house of ice blocks as a temporary outlet for his fire water.[45]

This first winter carnival also scored high marks for its freedom from accidents. Erecting so high a structure of ice was an exceedingly risky proposition given the frigid temperatures and the constant presence of glare ice on the scaffolding from the overflow of "mortared" joints. Newspapers in both cities reported a single serious injury, caused by the fall of a Polish laborer from the wall of a high bastion. The only other mishaps on the castle grounds instantly

A scene in the Indian Villlage at the 1886 St. Paul Winter Carnival, from a drawing by John Anderson

became a part of winter carnival lore. A Dr. Murphy ignited his nose while lighting a roman candle with his cigar, and a G.A.R. veteran became so carried away during the assault on the castle that he accidentally set fire to his fur cap, then permitted the flames to proceed to his hair rather than deviating from his pyrotechnic duties.[46]

Continued cold weather and a crowd that refused to go home stretched the first winter carnival two weeks past its planned closing on February 13. The ice castle still stood firm, its bastions slumped but rigid and its ramparts maintaining their fierce if no longer crisp outline. One more storming of the palace, this

time by the combined forces of the Ice and Fire Kings, led to yet another lavish fireworks display. Club tobogganers who had been absorbed in slide and float building or distracted with endless processions now spent their evenings on the runs, and skaters spread out onto a large, cleared area of the Mississippi River. One Saturday was reserved for another children's day, this time free for all under twelve.[47]

By every conceivable measure, St. Paul's first winter carnival was a roaring success. One hundred fifty thousand people paid the twenty-five-cent admission fee to the carnival grounds, and carnival organizers were pleasantly surprised to discover that, without

Skating on the Mississippi River during the 1886 winter carnival, from a drawing by Burbank

intending to do so, they had made a profit. The crowds themselves had posed the largest threat to the success of the venture. Not only were accommodations strained, but two of the most popular sports, tobogganing and ice skating, far overran the capacity of the slides and rinks prepared for them.[48]

The astonishing ascendance of women as active, independent participants in the carnival activities had much to do with both the carnival's success and the inadequacy of its slides and rinks. Initially included as honorary members of the leading sports clubs, expected to adorn floats and parades as well as men's arms, they performed their ornamental tasks to universal public satisfaction. But when freed of ceremonial duties, they asserted their full rights as club members or formed their own clubs, plunging into each of the winter sports with an enthusiasm as fierce as any man. St. Paul set out to exhibit itself to the world and ended up making some remarkable discoveries of its own. Society had indeed overflowed its bounds.

The last of the 1886 ice palace

THE MIRACLE-WORKING SHRINE

In a single season, St. Paul proved to the nation that snow and ice could spawn a carnival of astonishing magnitude. It remained to be seen whether so potent a creature could be cloned. Once the novelty of the first incarnation wore off, how many would brave below-zero weather to wait for a parade of people wrapped in blankets? After the social pleasures of the carnival faded, how many would hurtle down those slides of ice or while away a frigid morning traipsing through snow on a contraption made of bent wood and rawhide?

As the carnival organizers were aware, Montreal continued to possess a distinct advantage in regard to questions of this sort. Snowshoe, toboggan, and curling clubs were the ancestors of the Canadian city's festivals, rather than their offspring. Festive occasions had always been part of their winter sports club activities; neither the sports nor their social trappings were dependent on the recent carnival boom. In St. Paul, and Minnesota generally, it was quite another matter. For all of the popular notions about the state, its people at large had proven to be slow to adopt and cling to any of the

> "Never was the cup so brimming with life's elixir as since pastimes that bring exercises in the open air came into vogue. The ice palace is our miracle-working shrine, and hosts of uniformed devotees attest the marvelous recoveries that have followed their voluntary pilgrimages."
>
> ST. PAUL AND MINNEAPOLIS PIONEER PRESS, January 30, 1887

[facing page]
Ice and snow sculptures by Zeitner and his students at the 1888 winter carnival

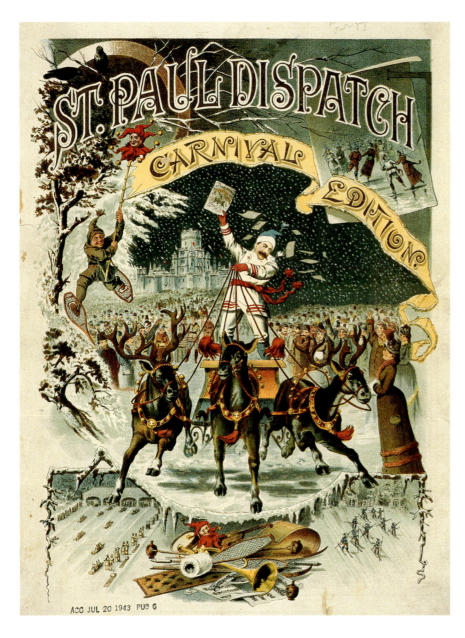

Forming sports clubs was the first publicly sanctioned step to assure that the outdoor games would outlive the carnival. Now it was up to the carnival organizers to find new ways to showcase them. St. Paul scheduled its 1887 winter carnival to open on January 17, three weeks before the resumption of Montreal's annual festival, and it was plain from the beginning that this time as much attention would be given to the preparation of winter-related activities as to the visual and pyrotechnic amusements.[2]

Once again the central feature of the carnival grounds was an ice palace, this time of home-grown design. Architect C. E. Joy, who had urged the hiring of the Hutchinson firm the year before, won a local competition and, working with the local contracting company of Taylor and Craig, conceived a structure whose size, opulence, and palatial illusionism outdid its predecessor. Planned in the form of a Greek cross, the new castle measured 194 by 217 feet and pushed one of its turrets thirty-seven feet above the 101-foot height of the central tower. That tower remained Norman in character, but it now took the shape of an octagon, its halls lined with soaring, arched vaults. Buttresses sprang from ground to tower, and from the point of connection turrets rose up the sides of the central mass. Ice blocks chiseled into a semblance of rough-hewn rocks formed belts around the towers, just as they would have in a masonry American Romanesque building of the period. A colossal, Romanesque triumphal arch, nine feet thick and sixteen feet wide, dwarfed the Gothic entry of the castle's predecessors in Montreal and St. Paul.[3]

Skating, which had been encouraged but given little space in the first carnival, found an enthusiastic sponsor in a new carnival association on the West Side. Capitalized with three thousand dollars in stock, the association retained two of its own members to develop plans for an immense ice rink on the Mississippi River. The lead designer, William H. Castner, was already a well-established architect in the city. His creation surrounded the rink with an ice-block wall varying in height from ten to twenty feet

*Cover of the
St. Paul Dispatch
Carnival Edition,
December 25,
1887*

winter sports of the early settlers, immigrants from abroad, or neighbors to the north. Until the mid-1880s "the winter was looked upon as a thing of terror — a season when everybody must shut himself up in his home."[1] The first winter carnival wrought immediate changes. Snowshoeing was born, tobogganing was introduced to tens of thousands, curling was plucked out of its Scottish closet, and ice skating began its return to popularity.

64

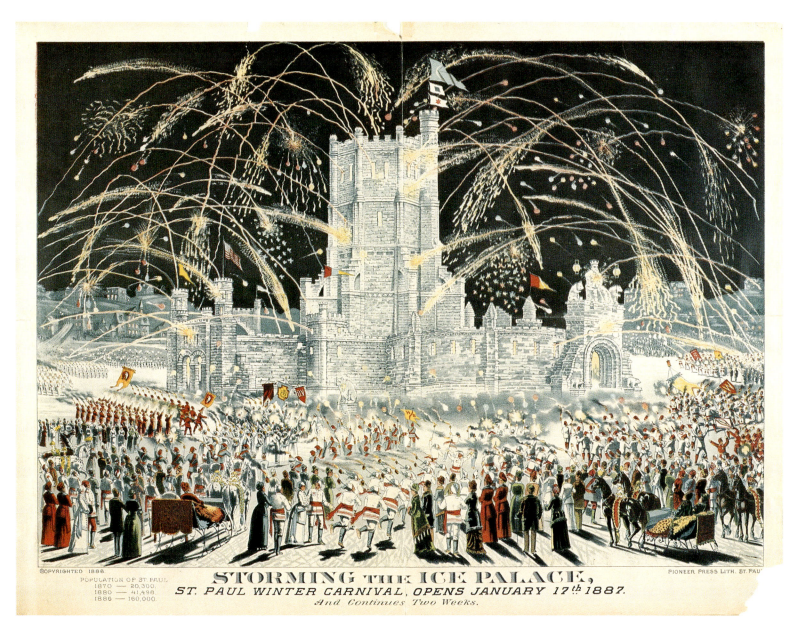

STORMING THE ICE PALACE,
ST. PAUL WINTER CARNIVAL, OPENS JANUARY 17th 1887.
And Continues Two Weeks.

POPULATION OF ST. PAUL
1870 — 20,300.
1880 — 41,498.
1886 — 160,000.

©COPYRIGHTED 1886.

PIONEER PRESS LITH. ST. PAUL

and adorned on the front with a bewildering assort-ment of windows, buttresses, and towers. Visitors entered through a grand arch spanning twenty-four feet and surmounted with a stepped gable topped by a pair of snowshoes crossed over a toboggan. Inside were men's and women's cloakrooms, a hot lunch and coffee room, a warming room with a fireplace, an oyster room, and, curving around the rear of the rink, a nine-hundred-foot toboggan slide. Even with all of

these interior accommodations slicing out areas of the rink, the enclosure still had an open expanse mea-suring 140 feet by 370 feet for skating, roughly twice that offered on the first carnival grounds.[4]

Skiing, at least of the downhill variety, finally appeared ready to shed its image of ethnic novelty. The carnival association did everything it could to bring it before the public. By this time St. Paul had two skiing associations, the Norwegian and the Hjelke

Chromolitho-graph poster for the 1887 St. Paul Winter Carnival

65

clubs. Both issued challenges to tobogganers, apparently to be worked out along the lines of their usual competitions for speed and distance down a given slope. A skiing contest close to the West Side skating rink pitted the state's skiing clubs, now grown to five in number, against each other and two Wisconsin clubs. In addition to Red Wing and the Twin Cities, Stillwater Norwegians had a club, and the unbeatable Mikkel Hemmestvedt had moved to the northwestern corner of the state, where he established a club in Ada.

The run consisted of a twenty-foot chute on an upper hill and a crest on a lower hill, which together would lift a ski jumper forty feet into midair. Prizes were awarded for both the best leap and the fastest time on a route that extended a mile past the leap. Hemmestvedt's reputation as a Norwegian champion in both jumping distance and the total distance of the run had preceded him, so his victory in each contest was of little surprise. As a youth of only fourteen years, Red Wing skier Oscar Arentson received considerable public notice for his triumph in the second class. Perhaps the single most telling feature of the skiing exhibition reportage was that none of the newspapermen referred to the Norwegian footwear as shoes. Skiing appeared to be a bona fide Minnesota sport at last.[5]

Curling continued to develop a certain calm popularity, its audiences appreciating the peculiar expressions and the Scottish brogue of the leading players

as much as the sport itself. Apart from announcing that the international bonspiel about to take place was the largest on the American continent, carnival promoters could do little for the sport but sit back and let the enthusiasm of the players do its work. There was still little indication of the sport's coming explosive popularity.

The number of local clubs participating in the carnival actually decreased in 1887, reflecting a reduction from the heady numbers established in the thrall of the first wave of carnival enthusiasm. Distant delegations from points north and west helped to compensate for local losses. Helena, Rush City, Bozeman, and Missoula, Montana Territory, sent their snowshoe and tobogganing clubs, as did Bismarck, Fargo, and Grand Forks, Dakota Territory. All were treated like visiting dignitaries and prominently featured in the parades. Minnesota communities also did their part, sending winter clubs as well as thousands of visitors. For boys, it had the lure of a circus, a place to run off to on a lark, with no thought of possible consequences. Three such youths from Duluth hopped a freight train for St. Paul, hoping to sell papers during the carnival. Their adventure halted on the fourth day when police picked them up in the street, shivering and half-clothed, and, much to their disgust, packed them back to their homes [6]

Though not precisely a sport, ice carving was as bound to wintry conditions as were the more vigor-

ous activities. It, too, achieved new stature at the carnival. The neoclassical silliness of the carvings on the 1886 palace grounds gave way to a consistent arctic milieu of polar bears and a conspicuously well-clad Ice King. Local shopkeepers, castigated on the previous year for resorting to tired buntings and flags for decoration, ordered hundreds of ice and snow sculptures to be mounted before their doors. Among the most striking of these was a perfectly transparent, life-size image of a snowshoer in uniform. Executed by local sculptor John Fandel, it halted pedestrian traffic before the downtown doors of grocers Kennedy and Chittenden for the duration of the carnival.[7]

Ceremonial events failed to reach the raucous heights of the previous year, as carnival organizers shifted emphasis to winter activities that would outlive the festival. Two parades on January 27 drew the most public attention, and neither involved the sporting

clubs or the resident Ice King-Fire King mythology. An equipage turnout displayed the winter toys of St. Paul's financial elite — Russian sleighs, richly appointed barouches, and ostrich-plumed ponies — competing for the road with an odd assortment of wagons and delivery vehicles. First prize went to a Russian sleigh trimmed in purple and gold, lined with bearskin, and drawn by a matched pair of black horses with silver-mounted harnesses and orange plumes.[8]

At noon of the same day, 175 dogs rendezvoused in the Lyons Block at Sixth and Sibley to begin their solemn march to the ice palace. Thus began "the finest display of dogs ever seen in the Northwest."

At least one newspaper report detailed every dog on parade by category, class, name, and owner, while devoting a single line to each of the toboggan clubs that preceded them. A judge recruited from Chicago declared a pair of Ulmer dogs, bred as boar hounds and having a combined weight of 250 pounds, to be the finest in the parade.[9]

For the first and last time in the history of the St. Paul winter carnival, the Indian village assembled at the corner of the grounds showed signs of rising above a circus curiosity. Its residents were encouraged to give daily demonstrations of the fragments of their historic culture that were still in place, including their use of dog teams and their handicrafts. Carnival organizers also directly involved the Indians in children's activities, leading or driving sledges drawn by dogs, moose, and ponies around the palace.

Living conditions in the tepees were still deplorable, but for once the press attributed the squalor to poverty and cultural humiliation rather than to some inherent weakness in the Indian character. The only moral defect noted, in fact, was one distressingly similar to a common trait among white men. As the *Pioneer Press* described it, "a couch of straw [is] covered with blankets (alas! for the days of Fennimore Cooper, when the lodge of the red man was carpeted with finest furs!) that are not particularly clean. . . . The haughty Sioux that in days gone by traded in furs and wampum, now has an itching of the palm as strong as that of his pale face brother." What drew the satirical barb of the reporter was a ten-cent charge tendered for watching traditional Dakota dances. For all of the signs of enlightened attitudes hovering about this second Indian village display, its central attraction remained the pitiful reenactments of what were once empowering communal events. Grass, buffalo, and war dances, torn from their usual seasonal context, now took place in the shelter of a canvas tent. Of the ancient percussion instruments, only the omnipresent tom-tom remained, accompanied by a motley band of horse bells, nail cask, and snare drum.[10]

Lighting and fireworks displays reached a peak at the 1887 carnival that was unlikely ever to be exceeded. Fifteen thousand gaslights, each covered with a globe in one of four colors, illuminated the streets of the downtown. A local gas fitter supplied each of the lights with a tin canopy to prevent the havoc that high winds had caused with the gas jets the previous year. For children's day at the end of the first week, hundreds of paper balloons, elephants, fish, and other odd-shaped, tissue-paper firework creations were lofted skyward, spewing sparks or exploding to bits at the end of their journey.

But the *pièce de résistance* was, once again, the fireworks display at the two stormings of the castle. J. S. Robertson, the man in charge of pyrotechnic displays at all of the 1880s ice carnivals, announced that the fireworks would be "five times as fine as they were last year." A battery of copper mortars, twenty thousand

Children waiting to begin their rides on dog and moose trains at the 1887 carnival

Roman candles, and a huge array of paper bombs and fountains were set off in seventy-five set pieces. Among the louder effects was the simultaneous explosion of twenty-four mortar shells. From a purely visual standpoint, far and away the most spectacular set piece was the sudden appearance of Borealis's name spelled out in three-foot purple letters. Raved a Boston visitor, "The illumination and fireworks were superior to anything I ever witnessed at a Naples fete or a Parisian celebration. It was the most magnificent and stupendous affair ever got up by an enterprising people."[11]

Difficulties in providing for the crowds had somewhat muted the tone of the association's enthusiasm at the end of the inaugural festival. The second carnival left no such regrets in its wake. Organizers and the media positively crowed. "Hundreds of thousands of people" packed the trains in and out of the city, and "a fair estimate of the number" of people witnessing the final storming of the palace "could not well put it at less than 100,000." The weeks of entertainment "simply illustrated for the first time what the St. Paul winter carnival was meant to be and to do, and it has fixed for years to come this unique and enjoyable feature of our winter life." Above all, it proved to visitors "what the breath and vigor of our dry and nipping winter air can do for them."[12]

Democratic in spirit though each of the St. Paul winter carnivals tried to be, they also strongly reflected the personalities and interests of their organizers. The president of the St. Paul Winter Carnival and Ice Palace Association in particular placed a strong stamp on the festivities. Under George Finch, an avid

The 1887 ice palace at night, with creative touches added by the photographer

sportsman and tireless socializer, the first carnival emphasized the formation of winter sports clubs and the social aspect of even the most athletic activities. When L. H. Maxfield, a man of deep cultural as well as athletic interests, took the reins for the 1887 carnival, sporting events achieved more focus, ice sculpture came into its own, and the beauty of each parade and display became as important as its sensational character.

The third carnival, set to open on January 25, 1888, also carried the unmistakable mark of the carnival association president. George Thompson, who had hatched the idea of a St. Paul winter festival in the first place, was a newspaperman who loved the limelight, both for himself personally and for the city. Under his leadership, the winter carnival became an extended exercise in showmanship, with the advancement of St. Paul as its primary object.

To a visitor, nothing could demonstrate what a city was capable of more dramatically than a street procession of traveling exhibits. The 1888 carnival had two knockout parades. The first was a promotional event for the carnival itself. The traditional passage of King Borealis and his entourage from Seven Corners to the palace grounds, still on Central Park, marked the official opening of festivities. Leading the parade was Borealis's float, which was in the form of an eighteen-foot ice floe. A Rocky Mountain goat and an antelope (both rendered in papier-machè) were placed fore and aft, and the king's spacious canopy in the midst was ornamented with an icicle fringe of plaster. At his majesty's feet, two *faux* polar bear cubs played, while a guard of ten bears stood along the perimeter of the floe. Six white horses in white harnesses drew the float, each attended by one of the Ice Bears. After the royal car came three others nearly as large, each representing barges of ice and snow. But the deepest impression was made by that triumph of taste and paste that initiated the parade.[13]

Passage of Borealis's procession along its route was said to be "the scene of one prolonged ovation," but it was nothing compared to what followed. On

ST· PAUL · ICE · PALACE · 1888
WINTER CARNIVAL OPENS JANUARY 25TH
AND CONTINUES TEN DAYS

February 1, sixteen thousand St. Paul merchants and businessmen assembled at Seven Corners to form ranks for the city's first industrial parade. Seven miles in length, the head of the parade at the carnival grounds was in a constant state of decomposition to make room for more tail at the other end. Dubbed "the greatest attraction of the carnival season" and "the most successful display ever seen in the Northwest," its purpose was one of unvarnished civic promotion. When appointed to organize it, William M. Bushnell vowed to show that "St. Paul stands at the head and front of the great progressive movement of the country."

Whether or not the industrial parade achieved its desired effect, it gave colorful exposure to both the history and the commercial accomplishments of the city. A full-scale reproduction of the first building in St. Paul, the chapel that gave the town its name, formed one float. Another was a cut-away schoolhouse, the front room showing an old-fashioned schoolmaster beating knowledge into his students' brains with a strap, the second presenting his kindly modern counterpart surrounded by "maps and globes and all the improved appliances of school instruction."[14]

Shortly after the schoolhouse float came a number of stunning industrial displays. The Whitney Music

Float and Ice
Bear escort for
the Duchess of
Minnesota and
her two atten-
dants, the
Countesses of
Rochester and
Mankato, in an
1888 carnival
parade

The guns and
sporting goods
float in the eighth
division of the
industrial parade
at the 1888
carnival

Company created an immense canvas mock-up of a piano, inside of which a real organ played as the parade moved forward. St. Paul Wire Works fabricated a sleigh entirely of their product. To St. Paul Roofing and Cornice Works Company belonged the most novel float of all: a great platform and pedestal of embossed sheet iron supporting a gigantic human figure seated astride a beer barrel and holding aloft a mammoth mug. This was *real* mythology at work, creating pageantry out of the express values and ideals of the young city. Coupled with the energetic boost-erism of the industrial parade, ice palace lore must have seemed curiously out of place.

Given the focus on spectacle by the 1888 carnival organizers, it is hardly surprising that the role of the Indians was this time reduced to a white man's sideshow. Two twenty-five-foot tents dominated the

72

Indian village, each of them offering views of the "dusky men of the forest" outfitted in a conglomeration of calico, black velvet, beads, and tin ornaments. Rather than leading the children around on animal rides, the Indian men marched about the park in war paint, feathers, and bells, a throng of boys and girls in their wake. Instead of demonstrating the relationship between traditional and modern winter pastimes, Indian participation now centered on a sham battle, using traditional weapons and fighting techniques, between the Dakota (Sioux) Indians already present and a band of Ojibway (Chippewa) especially brought in for the occasion.

Under the leadership of the Dakota leader, William Columbus, what could have been a humiliating exercise became a public ritual of pacification between the two historically antagonistic groups. The night before the staged conflict, he charged his people, "You must be very careful in this fight that there shall be no blood spilt. We will show our pale face brothers how we used to go upon the warpath many moons ago. But we will also show them that we have learned the lessons of peace." Encouraged to make the battle as realistic as possible, the Indians did enough damage to their props to bring the battle to a premature end.[15]

Construction of the ice palace failed to draw the notice it had achieved in earlier years, and the design nearly cloned that of 1887. The only obvious alterations were to the central tower, now built on a circular rather than octagonal plan and encased in a lofty but only weakly projecting bulwark. On the entry side of the castle, the bulwark had five large openings that looked for all the world like showcase windows. That, in fact, was their purpose, to display monumental ice sculptures as if they were advertising the contents of a store — once again, a mark of the carnival's increasingly commercial look.

However clichéd its presentation within the castle walls, ice sculpture was one of the highlights of the 1888 festival. One of the most powerful images of the carnival was a monumental, full-length statue of Lincoln wrought from ice by a Professor Zeitner. That sculpture by itself was impressive enough, but by the end of the festival it had attracted a dozen other carved human figures around it, all the products of children taught by the redoubtable professor. Twenty-five high school students arrived, hatchets and chisels in hand, on the morning of February 1, and by the end of February 4 enough contestants had triumphed over the slushy weather to permit the awarding of numerous prizes. The display of Zeitner's work with that of his students at the east end of the carnival grounds attracted thousands of admirers during the closing days of the carnival.[16]

Snowshoeing, tobogganing, and skiing events went forward as usual at the 1888 festival but without the energetic support and participation achieved in the prior year. Only curling showed signs of growth; that was to be expected, for prominent businessmen and industrialists had begun to take an interest in the sport. The bonspiel at the St. Paul winter carnival was touted as "the greatest annual curling event of the Northwest," and that claim may not have been far from the truth. The St. Paul clubs had so far improved their skill at sending the "spittoon with a handle on

Group of Dakota (Sioux) Indians prepared for a mock battle with the Ojibway (Chippewa) at the 1888 carnival

it" down the ice that they seriously challenged the Manitoba clubs for the carnival trophy. In 1888, however, they had to settle for second place and a silver cup, the first-place punch bowl going to a club from Winnipeg.[17]

By the close of the 1888 winter carnival, it had become a St. Paul icon and the association directors its high priests. "Rome has her carnival, Venice has hers in the old world. In America, Montreal has her winter sports, New Orleans her Mardi Gras, but St. Paul's winter carnival tops them all." This view was supported by the national press, which held up St. Paul as the natural successor to Montreal, in spite

and everything to gain in St. Paul's great assault on popular prejudice against settling or investing in the frigid Northwest. But the 1888 festivities sounded a sour note. St. Paul had narrowed the focus of its efforts from the state and region to its own mercantile interests. Agrarian communities in particular began to view the carnival as a way of enlivening St. Paul trade at the expense of the communities who sent their people and dollars to it. The *Red Wing Advance Sun*, an early booster of the carnival, editorialized "The abandonment of the carnival would I believe, all matters being considered, prove beneficial to the northwest as a whole."[19]

of the latter city's efforts to perpetuate a semblance of its earlier winter festivals. In January 1888, *Frank Leslie's Illustrated Weekly Newspaper* only stated the obvious when it declared "St. Paul has completely eclipsed Montreal in the manner of frosty revelries."[18]

Outstate Minnesota failed to take so rosy a view. In earlier years, nearly every community with strong commercial or transportation ties to St. Paul had touted the winter carnival. They had nothing to lose

Ignoring the signs that Minnesota interest in the carnival had peaked, the association pressed on to even larger preparations for 1889. Once more, C. E. Joy came forward with plans for a Norman fortress; only this time, it was to be built on the Mississippi River, where size was no object. The long dimension would stretch one thousand feet along the west side of the river just below the Wabasha Bridge. An ice causeway would carry visitors through a grand arch piercing the thirty-eight-foot walls of the enclosure. For the first time a masked ball, the carnival's single event to have resisted all efforts to put it out into the weather, would take place within the castle. In a final burst of hubris, the association determined that this time the ice palace would be kept open all hours of the day and night.[20]

The one piece of the equation that no excess of zeal or optimism could bring about was cold weather. After several years of numbingly cold Januarys, St. Paul once more embarked on a series of mild winters. The dingy mass to which the 1888 ice castle had been prematurely reduced was a warning. January 1889 brought the real thing. Facing a temperature of fifty-five degrees, with bare ground and neither cold nor snow in the forecast, the carnival association officially postponed the fourth annual ice palace and

LITH.
Price, McGill & Co.
St. Paul, Minn.

ST. PAUL ICE PALACE 1889.
POSTPONED TO 1890,
ON ACCOUNT OF THE WARM WEATHER.

Chromolithograph poster for the 1889 St. Paul Winter Carnival, published after the decision to postpone it

carnival until 1890. When that year arrived, another mild winter postponed the carnival indefinitely. Minneapolis skeptics had apparently been right all along: Minnesota winters were simply too balmy to support a palace of ice.

St. Paul's winter carnival had one last hurrah before the century closed. It is tempting to link the timing of this attempt at resuscitation of the tenuous tradition with an event of November 1895: a convention held in St. Paul to initiate a nationwide effort at increasing immigration to the Northwest. However, the actual content of the 1896 carnival belies any association with so far-reaching an aim. This time, it was plainly an entertainment aimed at the local population. In its lack of self-seriousness and use of campy decor, it anticipated the consciously parochial sports festivals of the future rather than

recalling the cosmopolitan spectacles of the immediate past.

Once more, the president of the association set the tone. William H. Van Sant was a man of society who knew the proper bounds of seriousness. His first proclamation as "Lord High Chancellor" (a title held with considerably more peacockery by George Thompson) was an announcement of the peerless "Queen Gloriana, Daisy, Corker" chosen by Borealis — daisy and corker being popular slang terms for anything or anyone rated highly. This was not your average carnival queen. As impersonated by one Andrew Heckler, "she is a new woman of the very newest possible type and wants everyone to know it. She was attired in bloomers of dark hue and a waist of Dolly Varden pattern, with balloon sleeves of enormous size. Her head was wreathed in bunches of flaxen curls, on top of which perched a hat of indescribable shape."[21]

Lest anyone think that the "new woman" was being singled out for burlesque, the carnival also sponsored a mock legislature. All duly elected legislators in town were called into a sham session, where the differences between the two houses immediately became apparent. State senators attempted a few awkward jokes, realized that they were out of their element, and promptly adjourned. In the house, on the other hand, bills and resolutions passed hand over foot, their sponsors convulsed with laughter at meanings known only to them.[22]

King Borealis, in the meantime, traveled about on a faux-winter float. "The car of the Ice King," wrote a local reporter, "is a marvel in ice and snow effects worked out with such skill that the blocks made of lumber and canvas appear really translucent. The base of the float is made to represent a large, flat cake of ice, on the front of which stands a stuffed polar bear, whose attitude, as he stands on all fours about to step forward, is most life-like and menacing."[23]

After accepting the keys of the city, the king immediately took aim at the modern man's digest of complaints:

We abolish all taxes and assessments.
We declare all debts, great and small,
  paid and extinguished.
We liberate all prisoners.
We declare all the sick well, the poor rich,
  and reduce the price of all drinks to 5 cents.[24]

The ice castle, such as it was, exuded a similar politic spirit. "Fort Karnival is an ice palace for those who want plenty of ice for their winter pleasures, and merely an enclosure for the purpose of carrying on carnival sports for those who do not want an ice palace." Built on Aurora Street northwest of the earlier site, it was promptly dubbed "Aurorapolis" or "Auroropolaris" — either name was perfectly suitable.

What permitted such a broad latitude in the way the castle was perceived was its incompleteness. Mild weather halted construction beyond the lower half of the outside walls. Rather than abandon the project altogether, the carnival association decided to run spaced blocks along the top of whatever had been completed, creating the effect of castellation. Those who wanted to see a castle might agree with a reporter's description: "The beautiful facade and retaining walls look like a fairy palace of crystal, lit up with millions of lights and shin[ing] and sparkl[ing] in prismatic glory. In the center is a mass of crystal towering high in the air, every inch of it glittering in the effort to permit the egress of the beams of light that fill all the space in the crystal chambers." To the less imaginative, it was a bare wall of ice blocks with some affectations of turrets and towers around the central gate, fully looking the part of a structure that had been built in a single day.[25]

Even the Indian "village" at the carnival engaged in the spirit of light-hearted caricature. Finally dropping its pretensions of historical or anthropological display,

Ida Lusk Holman and her son James tobogganing on a private slide in St. Paul, November 11, 1896

77

it relied on the services of Indian entertainers imported from Wisconsin. This time they appeared not as a
sideshow or an historical curiosity but as out-and-out
showmen themselves. Their acts burlesqued traditional
Indian culture in much the same way that a white
man whooping on a horse parodied the western cow-
boy. The actors were also admitted to be "rather a
good looking lot," in distinction from that distressingly common local travesty — St. Paul businessmen
who liked to "dress like the red men." Future Indian

acts at the carnival would be comprised exclusively of
the latter class.[26]

Only sporting events were treated with any degree
of seriousness; but by 1896, the proliferation of winter
sports activities in Minnesota had far outstripped the
earlier carnivals' efforts to promote them. Now the
best that the carnival could offer were echoes of
developments that had taken place without it. During
the eight-year absence of winter parades and other
public spectacles, the old winter sports clubs had all

but disappeared, their places taken by a handful of neighborhood and workplace associations. Remaining members of the Windsor Toboggan Club looked into its long-inactive bank account, found two hundred dollars, and donated it to the Northwestern Curling Association for the purchase of a trophy, a fair indication of where the interest of high society had headed. St. George's Snowshoe Club, once the prince of all St. Paul winter sports associations, had long since ceased to operate; now there was only the Sons of St. George, which sponsored euchre parties.[27]

After its early adoption by the upper reaches of society, tobogganing had fallen into the same state of unorganized recreation as that long enjoyed by the other and older (among white settlers) sorts of coasting. No longer dependent on the stimulus of the winter carnival, the sport drifted into back lots and farm yards across the state. The universal simplicity of the slide's design — an inclined plank structure supported by a wooden trestle, with a ladder or ramp to the top — spurred its construction everywhere there was a snowpack and at least one individual addicted to ten seconds of blurring speed followed by a five-minute trudge back to the summit.

In the meantime, other coasting devices abounded. Runners of wood or steel, patented or hand-made, could be attached to anything they were able to support. From the 1890s well into the 1920s, packing crates dominated the lower end of the market, especially as a means of hauling toddlers about. At the upper end there were patent sleds with thin plank seats, steel runners, and a steering bar. Handled carelessly, these sleds were the peril of pedestrians everywhere.

No longer able to introduce new coasting sports to Minnesotans, the winter carnival could still build a slide taller and faster than any other in the state. The 1896 toboggan slide, four chutes wide, soared above the castellated enclosure that comprised the ice

Curlers on the Raspberry Island rink in 1892. T. de Trulstrup drew the subject for an article on curling in St. Paul for *Harper's Weekly*, February 13, 1892.

palace, providing as powerful an image of carnival activity as the monumental towers of earlier years. The thousands who used it also had the opportunity to indulge in the sport under electric lights and in the midst of a grand party.

When the Windsor Club offered its support to curling, it was acknowledging that the sport had finally broken free from its moorings in Scotsmen's clubs. By 1896 Duluth curlers had become as devoted to the sport as their counterparts in Minneapolis and

St. Paul. Curling in Duluth owed its origins not to devotees of Robert Burns but to a French lake captain and shipping vessel agent by the name of F. N. LaSalle. Prior to settling in Duluth, LaSalle had spent much of his unoccupied winters wandering about Chicago. On a chance stroll through Lincoln Park, he saw a group of men hurling stones across the ice. Their sport so intrigued him that, on moving to Duluth, he shamed the local Scottish settlers into establishing a curling club. On Christmas morning 1891 the club, with several non-Scotsmen participating, played its first game, using a rink framed by the foundation of a burned warehouse and covered by a crude canopy of lumber and canvas. A late winter blizzard in the first year destroyed everything but the curling stones, but the club was on its way.[28]

Before the renewal of carnival activities, St. Paul curlers had already invited their Duluth counterparts to several bonspiels, all held on a lagoon next to Raspberry Island. The new curling rinks were sheltered within a timber structure built on stilts sunk into the Mississippi River bottom. Large openings under the roof and electric lights created a dim sort of visibility, and the sliding of stones across the ice was said to have resembled the roll of thunder. By the time of the 1896 carnival, the St. Paul club no longer needed the promotional umbrella of a larger festival to assure avid participation and respectable audiences. In spite of considerable hoopla concerning the new Windsor Cup, the carnival bonspiels were simply part of a long season of local and regional competitions. Foremost among them was the Merriam Medal, first awarded by the governor of Minnesota in 1890 and since then symbolic of the state championship.

A number of winter sports barely put in an appearance at the 1896 carnival. Ice polo, played with balls and sticks curved at the lower end, had never attracted great attention locally and by 1896 was feeling pressure from the somewhat similar new sport of ice hockey. Both were minimally present. Fancy skating was also a fading presence, not in the carnival alone but through the Twin Cities and the country at large.

After its raging popularity in the 1880s, the sport had nearly left the local lakes, and apart from showcasing the "trick skater" William Dougherty, the carnival did little to encourage its return. Skiers, in the meantime, failed to put in an appearance at all.[29]

Of all the winter sports, only speed and novelty skating showed their best face to the carnival. Six days of the nine-day festival featured exhibitions or races, and they displayed a range and a competitive fierceness that was utterly foreign to the quiet undertakings of the earlier carnivals. First in the program were such events as a long-jumping contest, a fat men's race (limited to contestants weighing more than two hundred pounds), and an exhibition of trick skating. The long jump drew an immense crowd when it was announced that a world record was in jeopardy. J. E. Andrews of Stillwater came through with a jump of seventeen feet, eight inches, breaking the record by two and a half feet. On the following day he broke his own record with a jump of nineteen feet, five and one-half inches.[30]

For all of the excitement over the long jump skating record, it was the skating races that stirred the most controversy and roused the highest public interest. St. Paul's most famous native skater, Harley Davidson, had recently moved to Brantford, Ontario, to work for a bicycle concern, raising the issue of his eligibility to represent St. Paul in the winter carnival skating championships. (The similarity between his name and the famed Milwaukee motorcylce firm established in 1901 is only coincidental.) Over the protests of the Minneapolis constituency, carnival officials allowed him to compete. The controversy died away when John McCulloch, a Winnipeg skater whose prowess had evidently not reached St. Paul ears, beat Davidson soundly in both the quarter mile and the five mile races.[31]

St. Paul business leaders repeatedly tried to bring the carnival back in the late 1890s, but a sluggish economy and unpredictable weather doomed each effort to failure. Speed skating, however, remained a passionate local concern. The city was on the way to becoming one of the leading venues for national racing competitions. In January 1899, after one of its many abortive attempts to organize an all-embracing sports festival, St. Paul won the opportunity to host the annual tournament of the National Amateur Skating Association. John S. Johnson of Minneapolis held the national speed skating championship for six years during a period when the same skater could win both sprints and long-distance races. Johnson coupled his skating prowess with a host of world records in bicycle racing.[32]

City fathers and carnival organizers were quick to blame warm winters for the collapse of the thirty-year carnival plan. They were partly correct. St. Paul's failure to erect an impressive ice monument in the 1890s shifted national attention to cities that succeeded in the effort. In 1896, both Quebec and Leadville, Colorado, erected palaces surpassing in size and visual splendour any that had graced Montreal or St. Paul. Leadville's architect was none other than C. E. Joy, who finally got the opportunity to design a structure without apparent budgetary restraint. Smaller ice structures went up elsewhere as symbols of strictly local midwinter festivities.[33]

But more than the weather had melted the carnival spirit in St. Paul. A steady stream of super-heated air from the offices of the mayor, the carnival association, and the local press wilted the inclusive spirit, broad northwestern perspective, and sports enthusiasm of the first festivals into a saturnalia of civic self-aggrandizement. In many respects even such success as the winter carnival of 1896 enjoyed was a fluke, a small glitch in St. Paul's already evident retreat from state, let alone national, leadership in winter sports and winter enthusiasm generally. The spirit of winter celebration had to pass through other hands and into other Minnesota communities before St. Paul could reclaim its title as the winter carnival capital of the nation.

Champion roller skater, ice skater, showman, and motorcycle manufacturer Harley Davidson, ca. 1895

THIS WINTER PLAYGROUND

As St. Paul's ice palaces rose in succession and the carnival association sent out its emissaries like so many pied pipers to lure the citizens of the state within its icy walls, a number of sports remained largely on the outside. Some, like ice boating and (by the 1890s) skiing, had stronger local roots elsewhere; others, like hockey and horse trotting, were still too much in their infancy to make a mark. Even curlers, though extensively featured in the 1896 carnival, had more important bonspiels elsewhere. All of these sports had a single thing in common: a following so devoted that the public exercise of the sport in itself became a kind of winter celebration.

Ice boating was forever destined to be the most localized of winter amusements. Bone-rattling speed through frigid air was definitely an acquired taste, and an expensive one at that. Yet it achieved a stubborn popularity that survived the worst of winter conditions. It could not have succeeded without the mutual effort of two quite different breeds of people. First were the men of redundant wealth with summer villas and yachts and no use for either of them when the lake or river froze. And then there were

"No matter how cold it is or how much the wind blows and whines, it will not reach you when you have got into this winter playground."

GLENWOOD HERALD,
January 12, 1912

[facing page]
One-man ice yachts on Lake Calhoun in December 1898

mechanical engineers consumed with the notion of making summer things work in the winter. The barouche with interchangeable wheels and runners was one product of this strange alliance; the boat that would run on ice was another.

The ice boat came to national attention in 1881 when the Hudson River Ice Yacht Club held the first Yacht Challenge Pennant of America. In the same year at least one home-made version of the craft appeared on a lake near Fulda in southwestern Minnesota. Widely separated skids straddled by a sail gave it the appearance of a primitive catamaran. Winona photographer Charles Tenney included a picture of it in one of the many editions of the Minnesota winter view series that publicized the blizzard of 1881. A few years later, another ice boat put in an appearance, this time in St. Paul. According to a January 1883 report in the *Pioneer*, "an ice boat invented by Mr. Curtis, Engineer of this city made several successful trips across the lake" — presumably referring to Lake Como. Forty degree weather precluded a true test of the craft's ice-worthiness, and on any account, no further record has been found of either of these singular boats cruising the rivers or lakes of the state.[1]

Nearly three years after the St. Paul engineer's experimental run, in December 1885, numerous ice boats skated about on Lake Minnetonka, marking the effective beginning of the sport in Minnesota. As described in the *Northwestern Tourist*, these boats held six people and "could travel a little faster than the

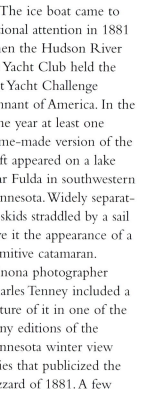

wind, though few will believe it until it is proven to them." The writer expressed chagrin that only six boats were out, "when there ought to be six dozen. It is exhilarating exercise, not dangerous, and if one does happen to get becalmed out on the sea of ice, the walking is always good. One does not run any great risk of drowning if the thing happens to capsize in a snow drift; and then imagine the novelty and excitement of going a mile a minute if the breeze is fresh."[2]

These first popular Minnesota ice boats were in all likelihood made by their owners. That circumstance and their capacity for carrying several passengers would have made them poor competitors against the Hudson River racing craft. Local ice yachtsmen had the opportunity to make just such a comparison in 1891, when Minneapolitan Theodore Wetmore bought one of the Hudson River's most famous ice yachts, the *Reindeer*, and shipped it to Minnesota. An experienced Hudson River ice boatman himself, Wetmore had eyed the *Reindeer* since its victory at the world pennant race on the Hudson in 1889. He immediately installed his prize on Lake Minnetonka. For the next four years, the *Reindeer* won all the medal and pennant races it entered, giving it a parochial reputation of being the fastest boat in the world.[3]

While the *Reindeer* was making its mark at Minnetonka, ice yachting put in a second Minnesota appearance, this time on Lake Pepin, a large swelling of the Mississippi River forty miles southeast of St.

Paul. A race on February 4, 1894, attested to the depth of the ice boater's devotion to his sport. With a thermometer reading of four below zero and a blizzard in progress, four boats lined up to start. Strong gusts of wind emptied one of the boats of its crew,

and manufactured boat over the best that New York had to offer, Minnesota ice yachting appeared to be on its way. Yet the Minnetonka and Pepin clubs remained isolated ventures, well out of the public eye. Later that year, Wetmore was invited to the annual

but the others completed the triangular course over scrabbled ice and reefs of snow, covering a distance estimated at twenty-two miles including tacks. A craft with the unlikely inscription *Cow Boy* emblazoned on its main sail bested the more felicitously named *Meteor*, *Comet*, and *Dart*.[4]

At Lake Pepin on New Year's Day 1895, the *Reindeer* ran against the Pepin Ice Yacht Club's premier craft, the *Tempest*. Ira A. Fuller, builder and captain of the Pepin boat, had been experimenting with ice boats for several years. The *Meteor* was one his earlier efforts and the *Tempest* his latest. To the chagrin of the Lake Minnetonka contingent, the *Tempest* won the race. With the triumph of a locally engineered

race for the Pepin Ice Yacht Club Cup, with the understanding that the winner would be the champion of the Northwest. He could not get ahold of a railroad car long enough to ship the *Reindeer* to Lake City, however, so the pennant remained an exclusively Pepin affair. In 1896, the *Reindeer* and the *Tempest* squared off again in a regatta on White Bear Lake timed to coincide with the St. Paul Winter Carnival, though it was not included in the carnival schedule.[5]

In the meantime ice yachting on the Hudson was on the way out. The last pennant race was held in 1893, and nine years later state authorities decided to keep the river open for shipping all winter. The yachts were sold at bargain prices, and winter sportsmen in Minnesota and elsewhere suddenly became the proud owners of world-class craft. Ice boats appeared on tiny lakes near remote farming communities, and Lake Calhoun in Minneapolis, a favorite site for summer racing, began to show winter sails on a regular basis as well.

Ward Burton of Lake Minnetonka bought two of the best of the Hudson River boats, the *Northern Light* and *Zero*. Initiated to the sport as a ten-year-old passenger on one of the hand-made boats of 1886, Burton had developed into an avid racer. His premier

Ellan and Andy Newman skate sailing on Crow Wing Lake near Nevis in 1918. Like ice yachting, sailing on skates first became established as a winter sport on the Hudson River. Supposed to be Danish in origin, it appeared now and again in the northern states through the 1950s.

craft, the *Northern Light*, had won the challenge pennant on the Hudson River in 1885, clocked at a maximum speed of 118.2 miles per hour. According to local lore, in a 1902 run from Excelsior to Wayzata Burton exceeded even this speed, traveling faster than any man by any means had traveled up to that time. Such a thing was indeed possible, for the ice boat could easily outstrip water-bound yachts, and aircraft was still a thing of the future. Only the fastest of railroad locomotives on a downhill stretch could have offered competition.[6]

Of all the winter sportsmen, ice yachtsmen looked for the narrowest window of weather. The ideal winter for him was cold early and late, without snow, and free of the subzero temperatures that, at mile-a-minute speeds, burned the face and froze tears in the eyes. At its inception, the novelty of the sport and intensity of its thrills put men on the ice in the worst of conditions. But this could not last. Snowy winters, harsh winters, short winters, and balmy winters were equally brutal to the sport, and the clubs gave up the ghost after the first two generations of ice boats wore out. Isolated craft appearing in and around the Twin Cities through the 1950s still attracted attention, but more as curiosities than as vehicles of a bona fide sport.[7]

Ski jumping, though shunned at the 1896 winter carnival, was well on its way to becoming the most popular spectator sport in the state. Red Wing's Aurora Ski Club held the first major skiing tournament in Minnesota, or for that matter the nation, on February 15, 1887. They called the event a carnival, presumably because it began with a parade and ended with a banquet. But skiing was its sole reason for being. Mikkel Hemmestvedt easily carried off the honors, while Red Wing's teenage boys "showed themselves thoroughly acquainted with the mysteries of the science." One of them, fourteen-year-old Oscar Arntson, took first prize in the second class, as he had at the St. Paul Winter Carnival the month before. Clubs from St. Paul, Stillwater, and Eau Claire all participated. Only Minneapolis stayed away, for reasons that were not communicated.[8] From that day until

the onset of the Great Depression, Red Wing ruled as the center of skiing competition in the east central part of the state.

Not long after the Aurora Club's first tournament, the Norwegians in Pope County began to hold contests among themselves. Every winter, as soon as there was sufficient snow cover, the skiers would gather at one of their homes, select the largest hill in the neighborhood, and mound the earth and snow into a jump halfway down the slope. Some time in the 1890s, the skiers settled on Mount Lookout north of Glenwood as their annual tournament site. Farmers from around the county gathered at one of these contests to see the famed Hemmestvedt brothers, skiing over a practically bare slope and launching their jumps from the same primitive launching device.

Skiing became so popular in the Glenwood area that nearby Starbuck began to hold tournaments as well. For the first twelve years of the century, the two communities jockeyed for national attention. Norwegian-American skiers Ole Westgaard and Oluf Jonnum, each of whom would soon win a national championship, participated in a Glenwood tournament in 1904, giving that town bragging rights to the first truly national contest held in that part of the state. In 1909 Starbuck erected a wood ski-jump chute and with Jonnum's assistance regularly attracted half a dozen of the country's best skiers to its tournaments.

Finally, in 1912, Glenwood erected a tower and slide that became the pride of the area for years to come. The enthusiasm of the local press echoed one of Minnesota's historic themes: "The people of Pope County have a Holmenkollen [their name for the new ski hill] of their own. If they would make use of it as they do their lakes in the summer the doctors would become luxuries." Upon the completion of the slide, Glenwood initiated the Interstate Ski Tournament and entered a fifty-year period as one of the nation's skiing capitals.[9]

Duluth was surprisingly tardy in organizing a ski club, considering the size of its Scandinavian population and the pride its most vocal citizens took in the

suitability of its weather and terrain for the coasting sports. Its first skiing association, the Trysil Ski Club, grew out of the local Norse lodge in the 1890s in much the same way that curling clubs grew out of Scottish organizations. Most of the early events used city streets and drew only local ski club members. For much of this first decade, Duluth's principle importance to the sport may have been commercial, as the Marshall Hardware Company of Duluth claimed to be the major ski supplier to the Northwest.[10]

With the establishment of the Duluth Ski Club in November 1905, the city's Norwegian sportsmen finally joined the growing national fraternity of skiers.

Scarcely three months after the club was founded, one of its members, Ole Feiring, won the national ski-jumping championship at Ishpeming Michigan. In the following year, 1907, Duluth built a towering chute in Chester Park, opening the way for successive assaults on the national distance record by Feiring and fellow-members John Evenson and Ole Mangseth. Five times between 1908 and 1950 the Duluth Ski Club hosted national ski-jumping championships.[11]

Skiers in iron mining villages north and west of Duluth scurried to keep pace with their city brethren. In 1905, the year that Duluth skiers formed an association, Norwegian sportsmen in the vicinity of

Coleraine organized the Itasca Ski and Outing Club. In that inaugural year, the club built a ski jump out of railroad ties, organized a contest, and drew famed Red Wing skier Ole Mangseth north for the first time. Four years later local teenager Barney Riley won the national boys' title. In 1910, Coleraine replaced the railroad-tie scaffold with one of the first steel slides in the state and hosted a national ski- jumping contest. Riley again took the honors, this time in the over-all amateur class, while Mangseth had to settle for fourth in the professional class.[12]

In February 1911, Fergus Falls, at the western edge of the state's lake district, entered the skiing limelight by holding a national tournament. Sponsored by the recently formed Park Region Ski and Athletic Association, the meet attracted champion jumpers as well as huge local crowds. First place went to Tollef Hemmestvedt, representing a second American generation of the famed skiing family. Skiers from Hibbing, Red Wing, and Duluth also held their own. The local skiing club so far underestimated the distances that professionals could achieve that they set the jump too far down the incline, requiring the best skiers to check their speed lest they run out of slope in the air and make a jolting landing on level ground. This deficiency was corrected with the subsequent erection of a steel slide and improvements to the slope beneath it.[13]

Technological advances in ski slide construction played a significant role in the rapid advance of the sport. Nineteenth-century ski jumpers had to shift for themselves, either by contouring an earthen slope or building a wooden scaffold constantly in need of repair and unlikely to endure the first winter blast. The patented steel slide offered at least a partial remedy. Introduced in the first decade of the twentieth century, it still required a wood scaffold, but it provided a trouble-free skiing surface and helped stiffen the entire structure against the twisting conditions of high winds. Communities such as Virginia could order a slide from Chicago and have it delivered and ready for use within the month.[14]

While outlying cities built slides and organized tournaments, Minneapolis, the birthplace of skiing competitions in America, continued to struggle to maintain so much as the presence of the sport. In 1910 Martin Strand, who would make his name as a ski manufacturer, built a hundred-foot slide in the

Ski jumping at Chester Bowl, Duluth, shortly after the completion of its new slide in 1907

89

suburb of Golden Valley. But two years later, the slide burned to the ground, and the sport languished for nearly ten years, until the Minneapolis Park Board finally took up the cause and built a slide in Glenwood Park.[15]

In the first two decades of the century, Minnesota skiing was thus firmly anchored at four corners: Fergus Falls in the northwest, Duluth and Coleraine in the northeast, Glenwood in the west central, and Red Wing in the east central. Zumbrota, Albert Lea, and Northfield had organized ski clubs during the St. Paul winter carnivals of the 1880s but, like other communities in the southern part of the state, failed to match the rapid strides taken by the sport north of the Twin Cities.

In 1899 the old Nushka Tobogganing Club took a page from the Windsor club and reorganized as the Nushka Curling and Skating Club. Curlers built a

new rink on Selby Avenue, the first to be located away from the river and in the heart of a residential district. Controversy over the refusal of the Nushka club to admit Bob Dunbar, acknowledged to be one of the greatest curlers in the world, led to the formation in 1905 of a third organization, the Capitol City Curling Club. By 1912, however, all curling interests in the city were amicably united in a new St. Paul Curling Club. Clarence Johnston, one of the city's leading architects and a bit of a curler himself, designed a building to replace their Selby Avenue rink, and the club went on to become one of the nation's leading curling organizations.[16]

Curling organizations in northern communities kept pace with the St. Paul clubs. Eveleth, on the Iron Range, initiated a curling club in 1909, eventually attracting Dunbar himself into its ranks. Hibbing followed shortly thereafter. In 1912 the Duluth Curling

Boys playing hockey on a St. Paul (?) rink, ca. 1910

and Skating Club erected a permanent building intended for the exclusive use of ice-skating sports. It set the pattern for similar buildings that arose in numerous Iron Range communities after World War I. The range towns became the state's curling powerhouses in the 1920s, Eveleth alone winning the Merriam Medal fifteen times in its first forty-five years.[17]

Ice hockey, that other coming ice sport, seeped into the Twin Cities from Canada. It was in fact a Canadian invention, based in part on English field hockey. The Canadian Hockey Association was formed in 1886, the year of the hiatus in the annual Montreal Winter Carnival. Montreal and Winnipeg remained the Canadian centers for the sport for many years. As the early St. Paul winter carnivals led to many interchanges with these two cities, it was simply a matter of time before the new sport established a local base. A twenty-one-year-old St. Paul youth named Ed Murphy is said to have organized the first hockey club in Minnesota, ostensibly as a replacement for ice polo in the winter of 1893-94. The first recorded championship game was played in February 1895 when the University of Minnesota took on the Minneapolis Hockey Club for the city laurels.[18]

By 1900 hockey had spread into the grade schools and high schools of St. Paul and Minneapolis. At the same time, many leading utility and industrial companies began to sponsor clubs, leading to an annual tournament to determine the Twin Cities championship. Just before World War I, Carl F. Struck, Jr., son of one of Minneapolis's pioneering architects, organized park league teams in the Mill City. With these three independent pools of sponsorship, the sport became accessible to all men and boys who wished to play and attracted an avid following that cut across social and generational lines. Though not included in organized school or league play, many young women also took up the sport. Many of the neighborhood ballparks of Minneapolis and St. Paul were regularly flooded in the winter to accommodate hockey along with skating races.

Duluth soon followed the lead of the Twin Cities in hockey, as it had in curling. By 1906 a number of northwestern Minnesota communities, notably Warroad, Roseau, Baudette, Thief River Falls, and Crookston, also boasted hockey teams. Strangely the sport grew slowly and belatedly in the Iron Range towns and villages that would become the Minnesota bastion of hockey after World War I.[19]

In distinction from curling and hockey, horse trotting attracted a band of loyalists belonging to a single social stratum — those wealthy enough to invest in racehorses and unwilling to engage in any sport that required removal of their fancy attire. In some respects horse racing on ice was the most fantastic of the winter sports. Rather than adapt the flimsy, open sulky in any way to its seasonal dislocation, the trotters bundled up and kept their carriage and its gear intact, as if the wind and snow were only a mild inconvenience and the bumpy, rock-hard ice a per-

Dan Patch pulling his owner's son, Harold Savage, and friends on a cutter, ca. 1905

fectly appropriate surface for the puny rims and spokes of the sulky wheels.

What made organized horse-drawn winter competitions possible was the invention of the rubber tire. Prior to the 1890s, winter horse racing had been an impromptu affair confined to snow-packed city streets and utilizing the small, lightweight sleighs known as cutters. Racing with these still survived among those who placed a premium on the health and safety of their horses. But the advent of the tire opened up new possibilities. Races could be moved onto lakes possessing systematically cleared tracks, and events could be scheduled on a regular basis. Saturday afternoon became the favored time, and the frigid occasions were quickly dubbed matinees, suggesting just another day at the park.

Around 1892 the first ice races in the state were held on Lake Calhoun in Minneapolis. This location soon gave way to Lake of the Isles, still largely mosquito-infested swampland in the summer, but by winter the most scenic body of water in the Twin Cities. Crystal Lake became another favorite Minneapolis site, while St. Paulites enjoyed the sport at Lake Como. During the 1890s ice-trotting enthusiasts and their equipage also showed up in such far-flung locales as the St. Croix River at Stillwater, the ice-clad Superior Boulevard in Duluth, and sundry spots on the Mississippi River from the St. Paul High Bridge to Winona. At Lake City, home to the Lake Pepin Ice Yacht Club, numerous matinees were held every winter for many years, one in 1898 attracting five hundred people.[20]

A sleigh-riding party from Almelund stopping in Lindstrom, ca. 1912

Supporters of horse racing on ice by and large represented the upper reaches of society. William Hamm, president of Hamm's brewery and the first King Borealis, and C. Milton Griggs, president of the wholesale grocery firm of Griggs Cooper and Company, led the way in St. Paul. Minneapolis businessman Charles Gates was said to have selected the site of his mansion for its view of the Saturday matinees held on Lake of the Isles below. By 1911 even the Iron Range boasted enough high society to engender the sport, with citizens from Chisholm, Eveleth, and Hibbing all invited to an ice-racing matinee on Lake Virginia. Enthusiasm continued on most of the state ice racing sites through the 1920s, the demise of the sport finally occurring with the expiration of summer horse trotting.[21]

Even the coasting sports began to acquire specific audiences. In the far north, a curious device called the *vipu kelkka*, which affixed a sled to the end of a long pole that swiveled around a central point, began to crop up among the Finns. Then there were the giant horse-drawn boxes on skids that served as the central feature of countless sleighing parties in city suburbs as well as rural areas. The basic principle of the bobsled, uniting two simple sleds with a long board, spawned innumerable variations, many of them designed not so much for speed as for the capacity to entertain a family or group of friends simultaneously. It could run down-hill well enough but as often as not traversed level ground propelled only by the flailing of children's legs.

Newspapers continued to publish articles and editorials reciting the urban dangers of coasting practices, but city streets, at least in the north, were by this time so frequent a thoroughfare for sport that sleds often became an accepted part of the winter traffic. In Duluth, the Rotary Club installed signs at intersections warning drivers and pedestrians of sled crossings, while city officials steered clear of controlling the sport itself in any way.[22]

During the period that the dominant winter sports explored various means of elevating their practice to a

public festivity, ice fishing remained a solitary, non-competitive diversion undertaken with little inkling of the communal spirit that would envelop it after World War II. It was as blue-collar as winter yachting and ice racing were blue-blooded. The practice of the sport was scantily recorded. "Went fishing on the river today," "men were out on the lake with their lines and buckets this morning," and "pickerel can be caught in abundance this time of year" are about as much as diaries, letters, and news items let on about it. Snapshots from the period reveal what the written word left out. Shortly after the turn of the century, pictures of men in fishing parties at lake resorts began to appear in photo albums and on post cards, showing that they were traveling and plying their sport together in much the same way as they did in the summer. In one particularly fine image, a dozen men posed in apparel ranging from hunting jackets to fur-lined, full-length overcoats, each holding a frozen pike about the size of one of his legs. Most seemed to understand that they were showing off a trophy, but a few looked

Eleven boys on a bobsled, location unknown, ca. 1910

93

A successful ice-
fishing party near
Pequot Lakes,
ca. 1915

as if they would be more comfortable with a gun or a
badminton racket.

Through the first three decades of the century, solitary fisherman tended to travel from spot to spot with
a variety of winter gear. Sleds and a combination of
skis and backpack were equally common conveyances.
For protection from the elements, patent shelters
became available after World War I. These could be
packed away, then popped up in front of the fishing
hole. Halfway between tent and canopy, they protected the head and back of the fisherman while allowing
him complete mobility with his fishing gear. More
often than not, home-made devices of sticks and can-

vas served the same purpose. For those of a more tim-
orous sporting instinct, the advent of the Model T
and other cars with enclosed passenger compartments
afforded both means of transportation and portable
shelter. Until the formation of ice-fishing colonies in
the 1940s, ice houses remained the exclusive haunts of
year-round lake residents, as they had been on Lake
Minnetonka in the 1880s.

All of these various uses and abuses of the winter
by irrepressible sports enthusiasts helped pave the
way for winter celebrations of quite a different cast
from the great 1880s showcases of St. Paul. The
panoply of properly attired and certifiably blooded

sporting associations had given way to an amalgam of scholastic, industrial, and civic recreational clubs, along with a healthy dose of individualism. Ice boating, ski jumping, horse racing on ice, hockey, curling, and even specialized varieties of coasting had each found avid adherents and distinctive audiences. If any or all of these could be shoehorned into a week-long winter carnival, it would have to be one of quite a different stamp from those that had gone before.

Ice fisherman hauling his gear on Rainy Lake near the Canadian border, ca. 1915

WE WANT THE ENTIRE NORTHWEST TO GET IT

O n January 27, 1916, the winter carnival stormed back into St. Paul brimming with new ideas and the old enthusiasm. "Make it a Hot One!" exclaimed the posters, and the weather promptly dealt its worst. New England milquetoast changed to hardy Minnesota fare on opening day, whipping snow and a bitter northeast wind against the faces of fifty thousand revelers. Undaunted by the challenge, carnival ringleader Louis W. Hill declaimed, "Men who cannot forget their business and get out and take part in the winter carnival are not the kind of men we want in St. Paul."[1]

To drive home his point, Hill promoted every exhibit and event of the carnival that he could lay a word on. He pressured President Woodrow Wilson to attend and, when the chief executive respectfully declined, pressured some more. He took the first spin down the Dayton's Bluff slide, formally opened the Jefferson neighborhood slide, and declared the Harriet Island slide "the prince of them all." Similar festivities attended the completion of the monster slides on Ramsey Hill and Cedar Street. Ten thousand

[facing page]
King Winter, first prize winner in the costume contest of the 1926 Duluth Winter Frolic

Louis W. Hill
in 1916

people waited in the storm for a shot at the former slide on the morning it opened. At the close of the first day's activities, Hill gave speeches, one rousing paean after another, to the carnival, the city, the people of the Northwest, and the world at large.[2]

Louis Hill was at least as interested in participation as he was in promotion. If he had his way, all of St. Paul would be on the march, leaving none but out-of-towners along the curbs watching the grand parade go by. As it was, two hundred thirteen marching clubs put as many as fifteen thousand uniformed people on the street. Survivors of the first three winter carnivals were said to be stupefied at the magnitude of the pageant. "Guess she's almost over," said a hopeful observer after two hours in the numbing cold. "Why that," replied his neighbor, "that was only the second division; we're going to have three more."[3]

The ebullience of the carnival president — and his infallible sense of the public relations value of optimism, inclusiveness, and the steadfast refusal to accept the impossibility of anything — overflowed into the carnival. One hundred eight candidates for queen came forward, and one hundred eight queens were crowned. Red and green were announced as the carnival colors, and shopkeepers and householders rushed to electric supply houses for colored bulbs. South St. Paul opened its doors, and thousands congregated in the stockyards for a barbecue. A poultry show took place concurrently in the armory, and the carnival brought it under its umbrella. The carnival association announced a trap shoot, and plans were put in motion to include girls of the best society and run the shoots day and night. Children's day was free and included

Headquarters
for the 1916
winter carnival

peanut and stovepipe races for those who were shy about taking part in winter sports. Three motion picture companies from Hollywood sent cameras and crews, and the newspapers declared there would be a secondary carnival audience of one billion people.[4]

Attracting a fraction of those billion people to the carnival required a new image. As an emblem of the increasingly modern, human face of the carnival, the ice palace would no longer serve. Uncooperative weather spelled its doom in earlier years, but this time the best of conditions could not suffice to raise a medieval fortress. As a practical man of affairs, Hill had little patience with romance, least of all a romance that put St. Paul back eight hundred years. The new center of carnival activities, now located on Harriet Island, was simply an ice fort, an assembly of ice blocks with little mystery or symbolism. No longer the inheritor of a tradition claiming roots in imperial Russia, its field of historical associations shrunk to the creations of St. Paul's own not-too-distant past.

In place of the ice castle, the association tied its advance promotion to a carnival girl contest. It was a

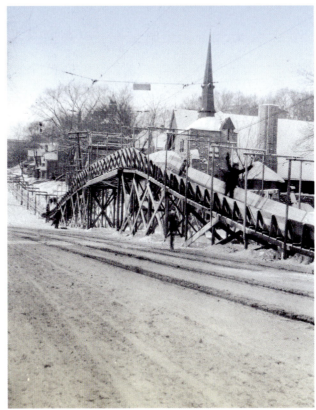

The Fire King,
Ronald Stewart,
and his Vulcan
driver passing
before Fort
Karnival in 1916

Two of the 108
winter carnival
queens in 1916

competition solely on paper, the idea being for communities everywhere in the country to select or create their own images of the ideal, then send them in for judgment by a panel of art critics and carnival officials. How many communities actually sponsored such a contest is unknown. But seven hundred artists, from New York and Florida to California, sent in their visions of the carnival girl.

As the rules of the contest specified no particular artistic medium, entries were as inventive as they were artful. One out-of-state artist sent in a colored sketch rendered in shoe polish, walnut juice, bluing, a piece of white chalk, and a red card. A local woman made a huge hollow cotton snowball open on one side to expose a poster girl on a toboggan. The winner was a St. Paul art student whose design was more conventional: a man seated on a toboggan, intent on the precipice before him, while the carnival girl faced the observer in a pose contrived to fill out the composition.[5]

The old Borealis and Fire King pageantry shed some of its more esoteric trappings, particularly those that set it apart from established mythical traditions.

"Borealis" lost one of its syllables to coalesce with Boreas of Greek myth. A drama that once stretched out over ten days shrank to an often-repeated spectacle of two well-known and easily recognized businessmen, one in an oversized robe and the other in a devil suit, going at each other. Humanizing what was originally a purposely mystifying sequence of events plainly reflected currents in American thought far beyond the confines of carnival festivities. This was a period of general debunking, when religious fundamentalism was regularly pilloried in the press and Masonic organizations were beginning to back away from their mystical rituals.

Bowdlerizing the Borealis legend allowed the carnival to retain a nostalgic link with the past while focusing the interest of the participants on the essence of the festivities: winter sports. Apart from tobogganing, still the most widespread winter activity, the 1916 festival offered a number of familiar sporting events: hockey, curling, fancy skating (once more a crowd favorite), snowshoeing (barely hanging on), skiing, and horse trotting. No particular attempt was made to import professionals or other well-known masters of any of the sports; the emphasis throughout was on citizen participation.

Less familiar and definitely less dignified sports also appeared on the roster. Indoor baseball, a minifad in northern cities, was adapted to skates, and a tournament was held on the Harriet Island rink, the Glacier

Park team leading the way. Pushball arrived from college campuses. Like soccer, its object was to get the ball between two uprights; only the orb was six feet in diameter, and snow and ice gave the game an entirely new dimension. Men and women participated with equal fervor. For a few days the horse-racing track at Harriet Island was cleared of trotters, and those inelegant contraptions known as motor sleds lined up to race. On the same site, carnival visitors were introduced to ski-joring, a popular Scandinavian sport that put men on skis behind horses and set them to racing.[6]

In keeping with the modern spirit of the carnival, the parade conveyance of the hour was supposed to be the decorated automobile. Much was made of the motorized downtown procession that carried King Boreas to his seat of honor, until the actual occurrence of the event put its sponsors into a scramble for horses. So many cars broke down in the subzero weather that the vehicles were banned from the grand parade in the next winter carnival.[7]

Motor sled races were the creature of quite recent developments. With the rising popularity of motorcycles and airplanes in the 1910s, an amusing array of Rube Goldberg contraptions appeared on Minnesota lakes and rivers, all in the service of adapting the latest technologies to snow and ice travel. One of the more peculiar examples transformed a triangular platform on skids into the *Ice King* by mounting an engine or its rear. On its maiden voyage sometime after 1910, this device conveyed its inventor, his wife, and their dogs down the Mississippi River from St. Paul to Hastings. Whether it managed the return is lost to public record.

Creating public races for such vehicles required some degree of standardization. By the time of the 1916 carnival, developers of the motorized ice vehicle had split into two quite independent camps. In each of them, a standard racing car body was stripped of its wheels and mounted on skis. Where they differed was in the means of propulsion. One camp favored mounting an airplane engine on the rear à la the *Ice King*. Relying entirely on the action of the propeller,

Pushball, a novel sport introduced at the 1916 carnival; here shown for the news reel cameras two weeks before the 1917 carnival

The *Ice King* on its way from St. Paul to Hastings in the 1910s

this sort of sled skidded over the ice in much the same way that a hydroplane scoots over water. The other group mounted the engine within the car, where it turned a rubber-rimmed wheel against the ice somewhat in the manner of the modern snowmobile. Each model had its champions in the carnival; which type of vehicle won the races was not reported.

To garner additional publicity, the carnival association hired daredevil Mink de Ronda to take a daily dive off the High Bridge into the river. Only after he arrived did the carnival committee gauge the depth at the open channel, discovering it to be a mere seven feet. To keep a semblance of the stunt intact, De Ronda suggested using a parachute, but while he was trying it out (and scaring the ice cutters below with what looked like a suicide attempt), the association canceled the feat altogether.[8]

The stunt story, however, had a coda. Three days after De Ronda's unappreciated leap, a "small man wearing a great fur coat and large hat" and calling himself Bill Brown walked into carnival headquarters with the offer to ride a wild steer for the public. A quick call to South St. Paul put the requisite animal in a wagon bound for the city. Once there, a combination of wild costumes, blowing horns, beating drums, and a barking dog so agitated the steer that he broke loose and headed for the river. Two minutes later, as one thousand pounds of beef on the hoof crashed into the water, the carnival association had its stunt. The unfortunate animal was pulled out, allowed to recover overnight, and subjected the following day to the spurs of Mr. Brown.[9]

Louis Hill and the newspapers exulted over the carnival's success, and the huge crowd figures bore them out. Sixty thousand onlookers pushed against the marching clubs during the parade, keeping them from performing the meticulous drills that they had rehearsed for the crowd's entertainment. Bitter winds failed to keep tobogganers off the slopes. Hotels and cafés did a roaring business. Only the theatres complained, their doors too hemmed in to permit the entrance of individuals trying to escape the bois-

A motor sled driven by an employee of the Great Northern Railroad at the 1916 carnival

terous entertainment on the streets. Two representatives of New Orleans coffee firms declared that they had seen many Mardi Gras pageants but were "compelled to admit that St. Paul showed the world something new."[10]

If the 1916 winter carnival was all optimism and high spirits, the one that followed was pure theater. Again led by Louis Hill, the organizers began planning for the 1917 carnival in October. The objective of so early a start was to coordinate parade costuming and performances for their appearance on camera. On December 31, almost a month before the carnival was to open, three thousand costumed skaters glided about before the movie cameras; a day later four thousand marchers in costume massed at the Town and Country Club for a precarnival pageant. Small marching units consolidated in order to present greater masses of color. One such group, the Northern Pacific Club, boasted two thousand members, said to exceed the total number of Mardi Gras participants

Cover of the 1917 carnival souvenir book. The slogan of the 1916 carnival, "Make it a Hot One," was changed first to "Make it a Hotter One," then to "We Made it a Hotter One."

King Boreas II (James Ridler) surrounded by youthful admirers at the 1917 St. Paul Winter Carnival

except on the final day. With five days yet to go, the citizens of the city had spent nearly three hundred thousand dollars on costumes alone, which amounted to one dollar each for every man, woman, and child in the city. The intoning of impressive statistics such as these was as important an element of the newsreel as pageantry of epic proportions.

Beginning carnival promotion late in the fall also boosted citizens aboard the carnival band wagon earlier than in any previous festival year. As the *Pioneer Press* reported it, "the first snow scarcely had fallen before toboggan slides sprang up in backyards and vacant lots everywhere. If there were no public skating rinks available in various sections, lots quickly were flooded, and throngs took to the ice." All this would be a warm-up for the sporting events on the mammoth slides and rinks of the festival.[11]

Carnival promoters and their spokesmen in the local papers traced the great lineage of St. Paul's winter carnival to the new year's feasts of Zagmuk of the Babylonians and on through the saturnalia of Rome, the festival of Purim among medieval Jews, and the Mardi Gras in New Orleans. St. Paul's mantle was said to be greater than these, for it covered people of all ages and classes, extending even to visitors.[12]

On January 22, five days before the festival was slated to open, the city awoke to a snowfall of seventeen inches. The cameras rolled. When the great day finally came, its program "put all previous frolics in deep shade." A break in the weather brought out a cumulative crowd estimated at 250,000 people. Thirty thousand costumed marchers lined the streets, a national ski tournament was held on a new steel-clad slide on West Seventh Street, and Como Lake hosted world record-setting skating races, horse and motor sled races, ski-joring, and tens of thousands revelers on skates. The cameras rolled again. Numerous stunts, such as creating long lines of skaters moving in serpentine fashion, were devised especially for the newsreels.[13]

Midway through the festivities, bone-rattling cold failed to discourage seventy-five thousand people from witnessing a procession of fifty floats illustrating the commercial progress of the city. A few of the floats may have achieved the artistry of those of the last generation, one of the more remarkable being a baked potato "realistic even to the steam and the square of butter" representing the Northern Pacific Club. But the real attractions this time were dramatic vignettes. General goods wholesaler G. Sommers and Company presented a deliriously incongruous tropical tableau in which its festival queen swayed in a swing amid festoons of palms, her attendants fanning themselves in an effort to keep cool. Far and away the largest float, a part of South St. Paul's much-bally-hooed ensemble of Hook-em Cows, celebrated the glorious historical development of the local meat-packing industry.[14]

The ice palace itself was little more than a dramatic setting for the elevated throne of Boreas, the Ice Queen, and their attendants. Its outworks of platforms and walls provided a superb backdrop for pyrotechnic displays. Set in Rice Park, the palace was barely a block away from the St. Paul Auditorium, where the climactic theatrical event of the carnival unfolded. The old bit about Boreas (formerly Borealis) and the Fire King gave way to a melodrama featuring Princess Pauline, whose identity was shrouded in mystery, as she disappeared before anyone could identify her. Ten thousand people thronged to the St. Paul Auditorium to see the drama's denouement. The *Pioneer Press* reported, "It was the crowning event of the carnival. Sensations came fast." Prince Paul, hitherto disgraced and placed in chains by the ruling King Boreas II, broke free and miraculously produced the princess.

When the king saw his daughter refuse his out-stretched arms and fly to the prince, he knew his rule was at an end. As Boreas prostrated himself before the new King Paul, the courtiers and subjects of the fallen monarch murmured at their stupidity; the Pauline of the carnival goer's searches was in fact the thespian king's real-life daughter.[15]

In between the civic self-promotion, commercial puffery and outright silliness of the carnival's planned

American boy champion Oliver Kaldahl of Glen-wood, one of the skiing stars of the 1917 carnival

Pausing before the Armstrong House on West Fifth Street during the decorated car parade of the 1917 carnival parade. The pause may have been more than a camera opportunity, as the cars stalled constantly in the cold temperatures.

Fred Hartman and his team before beginning the grueling Red River Derby from Winnipeg to St. Paul at the 1917 carnival. Hartman, a slightly built graduate of Massachusets Institute of Technology, entered the race hoping to set up a research laboratory with the $500 first prize.

theatrics came an event of such startlingly dramatic character that it overwhelmed the final days of the carnival. Hill and his associates had fastened on a long-distance dog derby as a device for engaging national interest in the festival. At noon on January 24, ten dogsled teams set out from Winnipeg to traverse the Pembina trail to St. Paul, a distance of five hundred miles. Continuous blizzard conditions, with temperatures remaining well below zero, quickly forced half of the starters out of the race. Of the five remaining, four were French Canadian fur trappers; the other was a young man from New York who had moved to St. Paul for his health. His name was Fred Hartman.

St. Paul waiting for its own to come home was drama enough. But the potentially fatal weather conditions, Hartman's inexperience against four seasoned mushers, his mounting catastrophes, and his unyielding determination to finish against all odds transfixed the state's and nation's attention for the last two days of the carnival. The American musher's plight was even worse than anyone realized until the race was finished. His best dog had failed to arrive in Winnipeg on time to be harnessed in; another dog was lost when untrained members of the team began fighting; a third became sick and had to be carried on the sled.

Hartman fought against his growing misfortunes by pushing the sled himself and going longer and longer periods without rest, defying one of the cardinal rules of arctic survival. By the time he was within one hundred miles of St. Paul and traveling without a lead dog, every step of his progress was communicated to the city by newsmen along the trail. He was a hero long before he arrived, and the fact that the four others beat him handily did nothing to diminish his stature. Hartman's name blazed across the front page, while the winner's column was relegated to the interior of the paper.[16]

French Canadian fur trapper Albert Campbell, his victory almost forgotten in the adulation of Hartman, was a dramatic enough character himself. His sled stood out from the others, for it lacked their back handles and side boards; resembling a simple toboggan, it was in fact a form of the old dog train. His participation in the race had begun in as theatrical a fashion as anything at the carnival. As he related it to a reporter, "an old fur trapper lay on his deathbed in a rudely furnished log hut at the Wood Lake post of the Hudson Bay company. Just before the death rattle came in his throat he called his son to his side. 'Win that race, my boy,' was his command. Two minutes later he was dead." The old trapper was, of course, Campbell's father.[17]

Not even a father's dying command could shift the public's eye from Hartman, however. Louis Hill put him up at his home, and Hill's children decorated Hartman's room with pictures. The queen of the carnival raised a fund for him. Offers of vaudeville engagements flooded in. A poem celebrated his exploits. And the *Pioneer Press* announced the begin-

ning of mushing as a new sport among St. Paul's "young America."[18]

None of the earlier carnivals ended on a more positive note that this one. Louis Hill, the mayor, the commissioner of public safety, the president of the St. Paul Association, and a spokesperson for the Guild of Catholic Women all agreed that another carnival was in order and that the one in 1918 would surpass even the dramatic accomplishments of the carnival just past. Yet these civic leaders were speaking into the teeth of what many already knew to be inevitable. A break in relations with Germany had occurred just as the dog derby neared its close, and the coming war quickly put an end to the city's second run at establishing a carnival tradition.[19]

In the aftermath of World War I, outdoor winter amusements in the Twin Cities largely followed their own course. Occasionally civic leaders used the term "carnival" to cover a hodgepodge of weekend activities for children. The Midway District on University Avenue sponsored its own sports carnivals as a means of picking up business during its most sluggish period. But even without these limited efforts, devoted

Fred Hartman and his three remaining dogs at the end of the Red River Derby

winter enthusiasts had plenty to keep them busy. At Phalen Park, a familiar site to the city's skaters, St. Paul erected a tobogganing ramp with a gradual enough incline to be safe for unattended children. Fancy skating returned to Minneapolis lakes, particularly at Loring Park. Hockey flourished in the high schools, engaging the interest of girls as well as boys. Skiers of both sexes and all ages frequented the hills of golf courses. The kind of snow and ice sculpture once reserved for carnival sponsorship regularly appeared in city parks and on front lawns.

Sporadic experimentation with motorized ice vehicles continued. Leo Morris, the proprietor of Six Corners Garage and Hardware Store in St. Paul, mounted an airplane motor at the rear of a race car.

Perhaps inspired by stories of what St. Paulites were doing, the Landby brothers in Warroad, near the northern boundary of the state, put rear wheels and front skis on a motorcycle body and breezed through the streets of the town. None of these vehicles posed a threat to the speed records of ice yachts.[20]

During the 1920s Twin Cities audiences for outdoor winter sports events sank to nineteenth century, precarnival levels. The real draw, as it had been in the winter of 1884-85, was indoor exhibitions — only this time it was ice skating shows rather than roller-skating and bicycling races. St. Paul had the State Fair hippodrome and its sister city a new ice arena. Minneapolis ultimately emerged as a major producer of exhibition skaters. One of its two skating associations,

Construction of the toboggan slide at Phalen Park in 1922

the Twin Cities Figure Skating Club, traveled to arenas throughout the region. Even more famous and widely traveled was the ice duo of Eddie Shipstad and Oscar Johnston, founders and guiding lights of the first Ice Follies. Their troupe of eight entertained huge audiences on the East Coast as well as the Midwest with a routine of intricate skating figures and formations, acrobatic feats, and comedy sketches.

While Twin Cities winter sports spectators confined their attention to fancy-skating exhibitions, the center of Minnesota's winter festival activity shifted to the northern part of the state. First to take up the flag was Eveleth, a young Iron Range city that had already established itself as a leader in publicly sponsored recreation. As early as 1912, the community had at least three municipal outside skating rinks, ranging in size from one half to one acre. In 1915 Eveleth hired L. H. Weir, a national expert from the American Playground Association, to survey the city's facilities and make recommendations, leading to a year-round program of school-sponsored recreational activities and culminating in a civic monument known as the Eveleth Recreational Building.[21]

Completion of the new recreational facility in 1919 coincided with the organization of the Eveleth Home-Coming Carnival, held in honor of soldiers and sailors returning from the war. The director of activities within the new building was none other than Robert Dunbar, formerly of the St. Paul Curling Club and by then widely acknowledged as the foremost curler in the world. Quite naturally the carnival, held January 1-3, 1920, revolved around the six curling rinks occupying the ground floor. Teams (called rinks by the players) from the region united in the first annual Mesaba (*sic*) Range Bonspiel, which would soon become one of the premier sporting events in the state.[22]

Ice skating also figured heavily in the Eveleth carnival. Although primarily an exhibition sport, short competitions in both fancy and speed skating were held for local men and women. A world-class speed skater, John Nilsson, put on two exhibitions a day, in

Olympic champion figure skater and St. Paul native Ann Munkholm performing at Loring Park, Minneapolis, ca. 1923

which he showed off his acrobatic talents as well. The climactic event of the carnival pitted Nilsson against local sprinter and ex-marine Marvin van Buskirk, who was to run a lap around the ice track while Nilsson skated a lap-and-a-half. Van Buskirk won handily, which probably had more to say about

William Pitt Shattuck, Jr., on skis at the Columbia Park Golf Course, ca. 1925

the condition of the ice after three days than it did about the speed of sprinters relative to skaters.[23]

Hockey received less attention at the Eveleth Winter Sports Carnival than the other ice events, for the sport still lacked any semblance of organization on the Iron Range. During the early planning stages of the carnival, however, a small group of local political leaders and businessmen established the Eveleth Hockey Association and put together a team for competition. Its first efforts were a struggle, for while Dunbar and the Eveleth Curling Club easily won the Rust Parker trophy in the carnival, the fledgling hockey team lost twice to Duluth. But it was hockey — and this hockey team in particular — that would soon bring national attention to the small city. In its first year of competition, the team went on to win all but four of its twenty-four games in a league consisting of teams from Minnesota, Wisconsin, Michigan, and Manitoba. The following year they won the

Minneapolis sculptor Nona Bymark Soderlin with her "Dance of the Snow Nymphs" in 1925

The Minneapolis Ice Arena in 1929

McNaughton Cup as champions of Group III of the United States Hockey League and soon reigned as national champions as well.[24]

Events held outside of the Eveleth Recreational Building proved to be a much less successful part of the carnival, for they had to cope with temperatures as low as thirty below zero. The grand parade lost its major attraction when the Glacier National Park Drum Corps backed out. Filling in were twenty past members of the high school fife and drum corps, using instruments provided by the St. Paul Athletic Club. Only one of the many out-of-town marching bands invited ventured forth. Ski-joring, or ski-ford-ing as it was referred to locally, had to be called off when no "suitable" horses could be found. Most of the dog races, with local boys in charge of the teams, terminated in dog fights halfway down the course.

In spite of the chilling temperatures, tobogganing drew crowds rivaling those watching the skating exhi-bitions on the new inside rinks. The recreation department had constructed a "permanent" slide just north of their building. According to a newspaper account, "a stream of kids from sixteen to sixty kept the twenty-four toboggans purchased by the city warm from the time the slide was opened in the morning until it was closed each night of the carni-val." Each of the elementary schools in the district also boasted a well-built slide, a sort of winter substi-tute for the playground equipment mandated by Weir's survey and by then buried under several feet of snow.[25]

When Eveleth failed to organize a carnival in 1920, one of its Iron Range companions, Hibbing, picked up the standard. In a move that anticipated the wave of the future in St. Louis County, its local American Legion post joined forces with the recre-ational department of the public schools. A contest for carnival queen introduced the festivities, a small ice castle gave them the proper historical resonance, locally manufactured carnival uniforms and a parade

The Eveleth
School District
toboggan slide at
Leonides in the
winter of 1919-20

of decorated floats and toboggans created the requisite atmosphere, and tobogganing and dog races, a hockey game between the Eveleth and Hibbing firemen, and a street jazz band assured that all tastes would be entertained. But the spotlight of the carnival through all three days of its run steadily shone on ice skating.[26]

The reason for the unusually strong focus of Hibbing's Mid-Winter Carnival was the reputation and promotional energies of a single man: Harley Davidson. Thirty years after his own best skating days were passed, he had accepted a post as assistant recreation director of the Hibbing public schools. Like

Robert Dunbar in Eveleth, he used the position to act as an impresario for his favorite sport, milking the friendships formed over a lifetime of international competitions to draw a stellar skating exhibition to the Hibbing carnival. "There have been greater skaters assembled for one particular event," he remarked to a local paper, "but I have never seen so many noted and great skaters assembled for all the events." The fancy skating headliners were American champion Minnie Cummings and two St. Paul skaters of nearly equal renown, Anna Munkholm and John Davidson. To assure that the skating races would achieve the same level as the exhibitions, Harley Davidson traveled to the Twin Cities, Grand Rapids, and the other range towns enlisting entrants.[27]

For all of the success of the Eveleth and Hibbing carnivals, they were not the sort of events that could initiate a tradition. To enlist the support of local businesses, Eveleth carnival organizers had traded heavily on sympathy for returning war veterans, and Hibbing's effort rose and fell with the fleeting tenure of a single man in its school recreation program. Wisely, neither festival was advertised as the first annual event of its sort, for neither would be held again without some less ephemeral form of motivation.

After a lapse of five years, winter carnivals revisited the Duluth and Iron Range area, this time in response to a statewide initiative once more targeted to dispelling the notion that misery was all that winter brought to Minnesota, particularly to those who had settled in the north. In 1926 Duluth, Hibbing, and Virginia each successively organized an annual festival. Scheduled to run back to back, they were all dubbed "winter frolics," a name that stuck to Iron Range winter activities throughout the 1930s.

Duluth's first winter frolic, opening on February 6, sounded a blue-collar note that would set many of the succeeding northern festivals apart from their St. Paul predecessors. Carnival headquarters were located in West Duluth, a predominantly working-class neighborhood. This was plainly not going to be an occasion for social posturing or civic strutting. The frolic committee invited business firms, clubs, and individuals to plan events or stunts under a single guideline — "most anything you can think of which will be interesting and different."[28]

Decentralizing the planning led to a wonderfully eccentric variety of events. Among the first to be organized were serenade groups, gypsy bands, clown bands, snake dances, pirate gangs, and "flash light peepers." Night hockey, Swedish folk dances, a snowball battle, tennis on skates, and horseshoe pitching on ice were soon to follow. As might be expected, the two thousand Duluthians who participated in the grand parade bore little resemblance to the tastefully uniformed sports and marching clubs of St. Paul's great festivals. Warm clothes were good enough; if

they had a comical effect, so much the better. Men in bloated white suits competed for the prize of best snowman. The major parade contest involved decorated children's sleds; no festooned turnouts or gaudily attired automobiles here.[29]

The three winter sports already popular in Duluth shared the carnival limelight: ice-skate racing, hockey, and skiing. Fancy skating was still not in so high favor in Duluth as it was in the Twin Cities, but a contest was held nevertheless. In hockey, Duluthians proudly broke a long winning streak of the Minneapolis club. Cross-country skiing, as familiar to Duluth as exhibition ski jumping, had not yet become a competitive sport; it simply took place whenever individuals or clubs felt like a run. The last event scheduled for the

Oxen carved from snow at the 1926 Duluth Winter Frolic

113

many pitfalls of winter carnival planning. National skiing events would not return to Duluth until 1940, with the completion of a new jump at Fond du Lac.[30]

The express purpose of this first frolic was to "sell Duluth in Winter to ourselves"; in the years following it was to "sell it to the nation." To accomplish this purpose, the frolic committee hired Jack R. Clemens, a former Chicago advertising man, to generate publicity on a national scale. By the opening of the second frolic, the carnival had been featured in five national magazines (four of them aimed at sportsmen, the other at general tourists), pictured in countless others, and filmed by three newsreel companies. Eight thousand posters of the carnival were sent out to railroad stations and ticket offices from Canada to Florida.[31]

For all the publicity campaign engendered by the frolic committee, successive festivals never generated the energy or fostered the citizen participation of the first year. Perhaps because of a sense that the eyes of the nation were upon them, many of the charming eccentricities and much of the provincial atmosphere disappeared. The 1927 frolic was introduced by a military salute, and each day began with an "Official Frolic Luncheon" and ended with a ball. In the following year, whistles and chimes announced the opening, and a parade of snowmen recalled some of the charm of the earlier festival. But by 1929, local merchants and businessmen tired of the time and expense consumed by the frolics and threw their support to a general, winter-long sports program organized by the sports clubs themselves. Even the "Ice Follies" that ensued consisted of little more than a local skating exhibition organized by the Duluth Curling Club. Like the first St. Paul festivals, the frolic had run its course in three years.[32]

The Hibbing and Virginia frolics were straightforward sports festivals from the outset, with none of the singular diversions and sideshows of their more citified cousin. Both began as last-minute local attempts to emulate Duluth's success. Hibbing also followed Duluth's lead in calling for local sponsors, with the roster of events to be determined by whatever the

festival was the national ski tournament at Chester Park, which had recently replaced its wooden chute with a gigantic steel slide. High winds brought about a postponement and ultimately a cancellation of the national championships, illustrating once again the

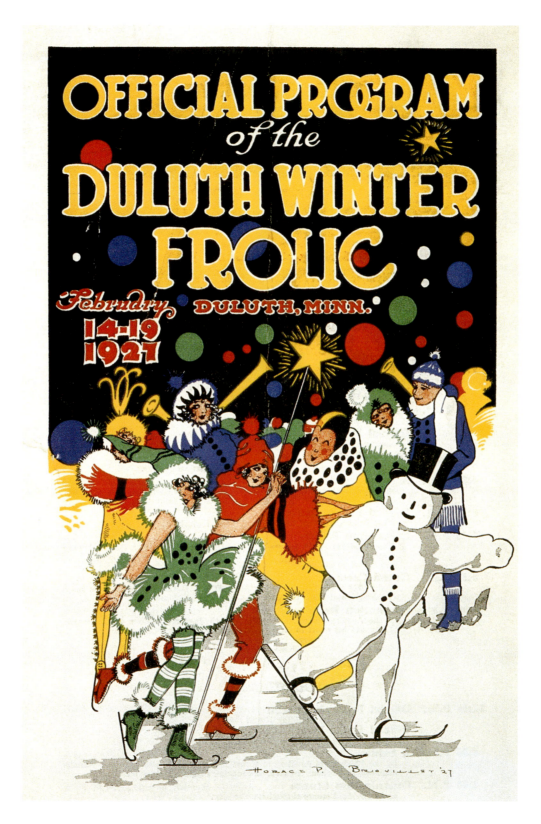

Cover of the 1927
Duluth Winter
Frolic Program

region's organizations were willing to support. One hundred local groups came forward, enabling the carnival association to invite St. Paul's champion speed skater, Everett McGowan, and the entire Twin City Figure Skating Club for exhibitions. The state hockey tournament also conveniently fell into the schedule, as did Hibbings's annual dog derby, then in its third year. Finally, an appeal to outlying rural communities to organize and publicize their own frolics on the Saturday preceding the main frolic led to a flurry of skating races, tugs-of-war, and hockey games, with the winners showing up in Hibbing for a final competition. In successive years, the Hibbing frolic became progressively smaller in scale. Completion of the Memorial Building in 1927 brought indoors nearly all of the events held in Hibbing proper. A year later all that was left of the frolic were one-day events sponsored by the surrounding communities of Kelly Lake, Penobscot, Kitzville, and Glen.[33]

Virginia's carnival committee promised to expand on Hibbings's activities, but they did so primarily by including gymnasium sports and promoting a contest for winter queen as the climactic event of the festival. The carnival opened with Virginia's annual dog derby, which by 1926 was in its sixteenth run. As in Hibbing, hockey, curling, speed skating, and skiing were the leading participation sports, and the Twin City Figure Skating Club presented the main sports exhibition. Enduring support by powerful businesses such as Oliver Mining Company and Virginia and Rainy Lake Lumber Company kept the Virginia Winter Frolic going strong through 1928. But in the following year, the community pared back to its old sled-dog derby.[34]

A year after its sister cities on the Iron Range had taken the carnival plunge, Chisholm tried its hand at a midwinter frolic. A low budget restricted its choice of exhibition skaters to the aging but ever-willing Harley Davidson and the up-and-coming Caroline Trask from St. Paul, but the carnival more than made up for its financial limitations with a number of novelty events. Foremost among these were a homely man contest, an auto backwards race, and a burlesque hockey game, the precise nature of which remains obscure. As in Hibbing, the original energies of the carnival drained away as the emphasis shifted to indoor events in the following year.[35]

While winter festival ambitions waned in Duluth and points north, a small, short-lived cry of winter celebration rose in a more southerly city. Red Wing, home of the oldest surviving ski club in the United States, finally had the opportunity to host the national ski-jumping championship. The honor had been delayed for many years, probably because the Aurora Ski Club had never built a tower for their slide. Proudly boasting of "the greatest natural ski hill in America," they had retained the reigning national champion, Lars Haugen of St. Paul, to design a slope that did little more than slightly alter the natural contours and add a bit to the top. The resulting slide, for all of Haugen's rosy predictions, never produced jumps in the two-hundred-foot range that had become typical of national competitions.[36]

Whatever the limitations of the slide, on February 3, 1928, skiers poured into Red Wing from centers of skiing activity in Michigan, Wisconsin, and Minnesota, which were then the principle skiing states in the country. To lend dignity to the event, Torjus Hemmestvedt, one of the original skiers brought over from Norway by the Aurora club, was invited as an honored guest from his home of many years in Thief River Falls.

Though only a single day in duration, the event attracted over twenty-five thousand spectators. It also spawned a host of subsidiary activities: ice skating, ice-boat racing, a dog derby, foot races, and the single novelty among them, a motorcycle hill-climbing contest. Most important for assuring that the winter sports day had full carnival status, the city sponsored an ice palace. Erected among civic monuments on the central boulevard, it added a spirit of historic solemnity to the occasion. But as it melted, so also did this one central Minnesota effort at raising a winter carnival in the years between World War I and the catastrophic economic events of 1929.[37]

In the final winter before the Great Depression, a few dog derbies and sundry tournaments and exhibitions sponsored by local sporting organizations were all that remained of winter festivals in Minnesota. As if already anticipating the bleak years ahead, such winter celebrations as there were forgot about parades, neighborhood festivities, and even outside sports, as they hunkered down in local coliseums and recreation buildings in oblivion to the trials and pleasures of the Minnesota winter.

The Red Wing Ice Palace in 1928

FROLICKING THROUGH THE DEPRESSION

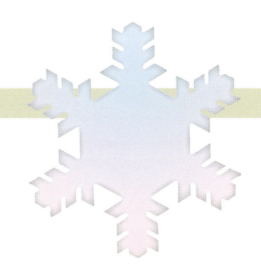

"**D**uluth will go outdoors and play," proclaimed the *Duluth Herald* in February 1933. With that cryptic announcement northern Minnesotans escaped the dim interiors of sports pavilions and once more marched, coasted, and raced over the streets and playgrounds of frozen cities. The weather bestowed its blessing by dropping the temperature to forty below zero. On the Mesabi Iron Range, the Ely Ski Club exulted over the beneficial effect of arctic air on the speed of its slide, and a local newspaper editor reminded his readers that "forty below in Ely is about on a par with zero temperature in Chicago and the lower lake port states." The spirit of winter celebration had returned, carrying an unmistakable Minnesota signature.[1]

Duluth itself remained hesitant to organize much in the way of a festival. Civic leaders encouraged a return to winter activity simply by seeing that the season's regularly scheduled sports events were clustered in a ten-day period and making sure that the newspapers publicized each of them. The true rekindling of winter carnival enthusiasm

"**Every man woman and child is invited to come and help in this Frolic. Make merry, the time has come to forget about depression and live again as we did twenty years ago.**"

PINE KNOT, February 24, 1933

[facing page]
Paul Bunyan towering eighteen feet over the frozen shore of Lake Bemidji in January 1937

belonged to outlying St. Louis County. First to organize festivities was the St. Louis County Club, which declared two consecutive Sundays in February to be sports days. Farm clubs in the southern half of the county had their sports day at the county work farm, and the northern clubs celebrated on the following Sunday at Camp Sigel near Biwabik. The county home demonstration agency and the regional Boy Scout council planned, publicized, and directed the events. Both the leadership and the geographic setting emphasized participation by the rural, student-age population, a far cry from the urban, adult male associations that initiated, oversaw, and dominated St. Paul's first great winter celebrations.

Perhaps the most telling innovation of the St. Louis County winter sports days was the care its organizers took not to separate sports champions from ordinary participants. No prominent outside figures offered exhibitions, and snow modeling, skiing, tobogganing, and skating all received equal emphasis, assuring also that the sports days would not lionize athletes within the county. A broomball tournament drew on people from both sexes organized into community teams just prior to competition. Even the hockey tournament occurred on a level field, as it was closed to teams already playing in a league.[2]

During the next three years, a third Sunday was added to the rural sports days, pitting the winners of the northern and southern county competitions against each other. Skating races and broomball emerged as the most hotly contested events. Coronation of a queen from area candidates closed the festivities. The winner, selected in part for her participation in carnival events, was crowned on a huge throne of snow and ice.[3]

A scattering of smaller communities in and about St. Louis County added their own distinct touches to the renewal of winter frolics in 1933. Cloquet in neighboring Carlton County initiated what it was pleased to call "the Mardi Gras of the North." Apparently the only requirement for earning the title was that "something will be doing every minute for the pleasure and entertainment of the people." To meet that objective, the Cloquet Winter Sports Carnival introduced motorcycle-racing on skis and public ice dancing along with the traditional winter sports, climaxing the day with a skating show put on by the Twin Cities Figure Skating Club ("some of the best fancy skaters in the Northwest"). The town newspaper boasted that two local boys of non-Scandinavian descent had mastered skiing and averred that one of Cloquet's own had invented the game of broomball while reading the opening chapters of the book of Genesis. For the benefit of posterity, the American Legion sponsored a picture-taking contest. Prints of the winning entries were displayed in the Cloquet *Pine Knot* window.[4]

Five miles from the Canadian border, the tiny hamlet of Crane Lake organized a single-day carnival on February 26 that reflected the French Canadian heritage of its citizens. Snowshoe races, nearly unheard of since the last St. Paul winter carnival, welcomed both men and women as participants. Another race required a man to pull a toboggan one hundred yards with a woman aboard. But the premier event was a dog-sled race, featuring not rough French Canadian trappers but local farm women who regularly drove their teams to town to purchase supplies and attend home-demonstration classes. One of them, Elizabeth Berger, lived sixteen miles away on Namakan Lake.[5]

The most enduring of the carnivals to begin in 1933 occurred at Eveleth, where postwar winter festivities had first opened on the Mesabi Iron Range. The first phase of the carnival took up where most of the St. Louis County frolics of the 1920s had left off — a January evening of indoor skating events. Shipstad and Johnston, now the most famous skating duo in the world, headlined the program. Skating races, hockey, and broomball games preceded the fancy-skating exhibition.[6]

Three weeks later Eveleth opened the second phase of its winter activities, an outdoor winter sports carnival in the city park at Eveleth Lake. Beginning with the traditional sports of tobogganing, skating, and ski jumping, in the following year it incorporated two new coasting fads, a sky chute (which propelled two coasters down a slide and into midair) and an event known as bump-the-bumps. The latter apparently had an artistic dimension, for prizes were awarded for form as well as number of bumps.[7]

In 1935, indoor and outdoor events coalesced in the Eveleth Winter Sports Frolic. Its date fixed at the second Sunday of February, this frolic became an annual event that survived in much the same form until World War II put a halt to winter carnivals everywhere. After a brief hiatus, fancy-skating exhibitions returned in 1936. By that time they had fallen under the spell of Broadway and Hollywood, as intricate skating figures gave way to group formations and elaborate set pieces. Frank Sullivan, formerly a local skating instructor and subsequently the headliner of a traveling company, climaxed his program with a bullfight on ice. In the meantime, outside events at the city park survived the brutal winters of the mid-1930s, but just barely. In an effort to keep frolickers from fleeing to the comfort of a home fire, the carnival committee lit huge bonfires at the edge of the lake.[8]

During the late 1930s, participation in the Eveleth Winter Frolic rose and fell with the success of the ice show. Frank Sullivan and his troupe became fixtures while other events slowly retreated into the shadows or left their carnival venue. The 1938 crowd packed the town's hippodrome. For ten cents apiece, twenty-five hundred spectators saw twenty acts performed by the Duluth Curling and Skating Club, Sullivan's new twenty-five-member troupe. Attendance fell off dramatically thereafter, as did participation in outside sports. In 1941, the last year of winter festivities, the junior chamber of commerce elected not to organize an outside sport program, while the Ice Follies were presented by a group from Chisholm, a neighboring town that had gradually supplanted Eveleth as the capital of northern Minnesota winter festivities.

The fifty-one below temperatures that had nearly jettisoned the Eveleth Winter Sports Frolic in 1935

Shipstad and Johnston, Ice Follies entertainers during the Great Depression.

were apparently an inspiration to Chisholm. On February 7, two weeks following the cold snap, the junior chamber of commerce announced a three-day fête to begin with a dog derby on Washington's birthday. The rebirth of the Chisholm Winter Frolic was consciously and pointedly connected to a nationwide renewal of economic hope. In a tribute to the American president whose messages and programs spelled out that hope, Virginia sculptor Duane Bryers carved a snow statue of Franklin Roosevelt near the community building.

Succeeding years witnessed the expansion of the Chisholm Winter Frolic into a countywide event. In the frolic's second year, seventy-five communities developed at least the rudiments of festivals, complete with winter sports queens. In 1937, as the Greater Rural St. Louis County Winter Frolic, it absorbed the farm-based constituency of the county bureau winter sports days. Placing the county festival in the hands of the rural schools extension division rather than local farm clubs vastly expanded participation, for it no longer depended on local initiative alone. The number of participating communities swelled to 100, then to 118 in 1938, the climatic year of the rural frolic, when more than ten thousand people were reported to have participated.[9]

Several of the "provinces" asserted their Finnish heritage by hosting events recalling the winter festival known as Laskiainen in their native land. Beginning with a morning program of Finnish songs and readings, the day ended with outside play and sports competition. The *vipu kelkka* or swivel-sled was one of the main attractions for younger children. In another sport distinctive of the Laskiainen, two children straddled opposite ends of an elevated log and tried to knock each other off with stuffed bags. A high-spirited Laskiainen organized by the community of Cherry pitted bus drivers against teachers in men's broomball, teachers against mothers in women's broomball, and held an open competition in skiing. Though each was community-planned, these festivals were open to anyone in the county who wished to attend. At least one, the Laskiainen at Toivola, was at

Children playing on the vipu kelk-ka, or swivel-sled, at a Laskiainen in Toivola

least partially funded by a government work-relief program.[10]

Rather than restart their own winter frolics, Hibbing, Virginia, and Duluth enthusiastically participated in the climactic festivities of the rural winter frolic at Chisholm. A caravan of 238 automobiles, sporting varying degrees of decoration, stretched out over a mile to carry Hibbing residents to Chisholm in 1938. Billed as "the greatest display of intercity amity the Range has ever seen," the parade of cars was preceded and followed by musicians and clowns that spilled out of buses near the end of the six-mile route. By the time of its arrival, the auto parade had, however, been upstaged by a "snow train" carrying 571 passengers from Duluth and the southern part of the county. All joined in a furious day and a half of skating, ski-joring, snowshoeing, snow modeling, wood chopping, log sawing, and "two score other contests of one kind and another." After crowning the Queen of Rural St. Louis County, the frolic awarded activity titles to twenty-seven rural girls representing each of the winter sports at the festivities. Their titles indicate such marginal sporting activities as "winter kodakery" and "auto-tobogganing," along with the mysterious winter diversion (or typographical blunder) of "spark stotting." Ice fishing also put in one of its earliest recorded appearances as a sports event.[11]

Rural sports frolics continued to enliven St. Louis County winters until the onset of World War II, but they never quite reached the height of the 1938 festival. A blizzard in February 1939 lowered rural participation, while the celebration in Chisholm limped forward. In the following year Virginia hosted the closing events for the first time, and most of the sports activities took place in a single afternoon. The gradual diminution of the Greater Rural St. Louis County Winter Frolic, like that of the Eveleth Winter Sports Frolic, could take nothing from its extraordinary achievement. In a time of economic distress and through some of the most trying Minnesota winters on record, each had managed to survive twice as long as any preceding winter festival in the state.[12]

As the St. Louis County winter sports carnivals and their crowds waxed and waned, Duane Bryers continued his solitary pursuit of memorializing great Americans by carving monumental busts out of packed snow. His tools were a pick, a sidewalk scraper, and a hatchet. Working under the auspices of a variety of civic organizations and service clubs, he produced at least one figure a year, each taking about ten days to complete. In Bryers's hometown of Virginia, George Washington received his due in 1936, then the sculptor moved on to contemporary subjects. Hibbing's service clubs memorialized Will Rogers in 1937, and a bust of Amelia Earhart went up before Virginia's Roosevelt High School in 1938.[13]

Attempts of other northern Minnesota cities to stage winter festivals during the Great Depression met with varying degrees of success. Brainerd's halting

Snow sculpture of Amelia Earhart in Virginia, created by Duane Bryers in 1938, the year of Earhart's death

to the games, the town was too worn out by the event to attempt it again.[14]

Only one other outstate sports festival approached the level of the winter celebrations in St. Louis County: the Paul Bunyan Winter Carnival in Bemidji. As early as 1932, civic leaders and school teachers in Bemidji organized winter carnivals around sports events, even constructing a simple ice palace to draw attention to the games. Introduced by an indoor event, the annual basketball game between St. Cloud State Teachers' College and a team of local school-teachers, the festival included broomball, a fancy-skating demonstration and contest, a dog derby, a curling demonstration, a hockey game, and skiing, skating, and horse-drawn chariot races. Enthusiasm waned after two years, only to be resurrected by one of the most spirited winter carnivals in the history of the state.[15]

At the center of the renewed Bemidji revelries stood mythical logging king Paul Bunyan in the form of a towering steel and concrete image. Set on the shore of Lake Bemidji, its completion in January 1937 gave the winter carnival that ensued an image with vast promotional potential. The creators of the eighteen-foot statue, Cyril Dickinson and workers from his lumber company, at first regretted its blocky neck and shoulders, the result of poor lighting and cramped working conditions. But Cyril's brother Leonard, as president of the local chamber of commerce, took a larger view. Paul was an unusual character and *deserved* unusual proportions.[16]

Bemidji's monument and the winter celebration that took place at its foot froze a wandering national folk hero onto Minnesota soil. A century of logging camp yarns had collected around the mythical figure, locating his exploits wherever pine was king, from French Canada and Maine to the Pacific Northwest. But Minnesota had staked a claim to literary priority with the publication in 1914 of a brochure written by William B. Laughed, a Red River Lumber Company employee in Akeley. As it happens, Akeley was only forty miles south of Bemidji, and while Bemidji was erecting its great folk monument, the brochure was

Start of the dog derby at the Brainerd Winter Sports Carnival in January 1935

efforts typified the difficulties. The town's festival organizers began simply enough, with a one-day sports festival containing a parade, skating exhibitions and races, and a children's dog derby. That humble beginning proved fortuitous, for the allotted day fell at the onset of the horrific cold wave of January 1935. Bottoming out at forty-two below zero, Brainerd temperatures rivaled those of the Iron Ranges. Most of the events were held, but many had so few regis-trants that prizes remained unawarded. Holding back the carnival until February in the following year proved to be little help, for once more frigid weather intervened and postponed the festivities until the end of the month. Although all four days of the schedule were completed and St. Cloud sent a large delegation

pulling, and log chopping, sawing, skidding, and loading. A cook shack on the lake front offered Sourdough Sam's bounty of flapjacks, maple syrup, sausages, and coffee. The public was invited to ski-jor on the lake, and skiing, tobogganing, and skating all took place in close proximity to Paul's logging camp and Sourdough Sam's victuals. In its final year, the festival added King of the Lumberjacks to the conventional carnival royalty. Instead of choosing a prominent local personality, a group of veteran loggers (the Lumberjack's Last Man Club) chose an eighty-six-year-old woodsman named Patrick Donovan King.[19]

Bemidji's sports carnival was also unique in drawing on the resources of so many public agencies and programs. Starting in 1938, the U.S. Forest Service, Minnesota Forest Service, Civilian Conservation Corps, Consolidated Indian Agencies, Minnesota

Babe the Blue Ox astride the International truck that hauled her around in 1937

still being circulated throughout the country as a company advertisement.[17]

When the carnival opened on January 14, 1937, Duluth and Brainerd, whose own efforts at Depression Era winter festivals had fallen by the wayside, sent special trains. In ensuing years, Hibbing and International Falls also sponsored chartered buses or trains. Paul's inseparable companion, Babe the Blue Ox, met the guests at the station. Constructed out of blue strips of canvas pasted together in papier-mâché fashion, Babe flashed red light out of her tail-light eyes and endangered overhead power lines with her long horns. Her legs straddled the International truck that motored her down the streets, spewing its exhaust through her nostrils. Radio stations in Fargo, Des Moines, and Chicago kept the Midwest posted on the events, for whom they were likely to be as alien as Paul and Babe.[18]

In its four-year run, the Paul Bunyan Winter Carnival marked out new territory for Minnesota winter festivals. Capitalizing on the industry that made Bemidji, an afternoon was given over to a lumberjack contest, complete with tree felling, team

Paul Bunyan Winter Carnival Queen Katherine Diedrich with Paul's ax in 1937

125

Highway Department, and Minnesota Conservation Department all prepared educational exhibits for the event, highlighting the natural and historic resources of the Bemidji area. In 1939 sculptors employed under the auspices of the WPA created monumental figures of Babe and Paul at the entrance to the Fireplace of States Building, while more WPA workers installed historical exhibits within. Coronation of the carnival queen took place before an ice throne designed and constructed by the CCC under the auspices of the U.S. Forest Service. Declared to be "an

architectural masterpiece," it was backed by a grove of spruce trees and illuminated with electric lights. Even the flowing, velvet robes of the queen and her attendants were a WPA sewing project.[20]

Of the usual winter sports, skating held the premier position throughout the run of the festival. In the first year, the city hosted the International Speed Skating Championships and staged an ice follies on the closing night. The latter event became increasingly elaborate in successive years, until it dwarfed the productions of Frank Sullivan's troupe in Eveleth. The

Bemidji Elks Band standing on the ice throne of the 1939 Paul Bunyan Winter Carnival

public was invited to participate in a masquerade on skates, which by 1939 had earned the local sobriquet of Mardi Gras on Ice. Of the many ice shows invited to the carnival, the Arctic Girls Skating Club made the deepest impression. Comprised of skaters from Nova Scotia, Labrador, and Iceland, the Arctic Girls performed such feats as diving through a barrel suspended three feet above the ice. One of the spinning acts was claimed to be "the finest reducing exercise yet heard of."[21]

The Paul Bunyan Winter Carnival continued to be innovatively planned and energetically run throughout its tenure. An ice map of the United States two hundred feet wide and one hundred feet long sheathed the court in front of the ice throne when the latter was recarved in 1940. Model airplane contests introduced in 1939 metamorphosed into live airplane rides the following year. A two-team curling exhibition in the first year expanded to a forty-team bonspiel in the last. When its four-year run came to an end with the 1940 festivities, the Paul Bunyan Winter Carnival could proudly claim that it left the stage with all its powers to entertain and captivate intact. Few other winter celebrations of more than one year's longevity could make such a claim.

In the middle years of the Great Depression, both St. Paul and Minneapolis responded to the revival of interest in outdoor winter sports by staging events that they called sports weeks or festivals, but none was much more than a single-week scheduling of events independently organized at far-flung locales. A St. Paul ski tournament at Mounds Park in 1935, for example, ran concurrently with a skating show at the State Fair Hippodrome and tobogganing contests at Highland and Phalen Parks. On a less formal basis, Loring Park continued to be a favorite Minneapolis haunt of fancy skaters and snow sculptors, as Como Park attracted similar winter activities, along with world-class skating races, to St. Paul.[22]

Construction of a racing track at Powderhorn Park in Minneapolis raised skating spectatorship to winter-carnival levels of enthusiasm. In 1932, twelve-year-old

Snow sculpture of an Indian, horse, and council ring at Loring Park, Minneapolis, in 1932

skater Kenny Bartholomew began his rise to national and Olympic fame by winning the Twin Cities Championship Silver Skates trophy on Powderhorn Lake. More than one hundred thousand Minnesotans attended the various meets held in 1934, climaxed by the National Amateur Speed Skating races. In the following year, tryouts for the 1936 Olympics attracted similar crowds.[23]

Only ski jumping could vie with speed skating as an outdoor winter spectator sport. The slide at

A snow dinosaur in south Minneapolis in 1935

127

Glenwood Park was razed in 1935, and an all-steel scaffold arose at Bush Lake south of Minneapolis to replace it. Modeled after the Lake Placid jump in New York, the new slide measured 100 feet up from the base and 160 feet down from the takeoff, creating a total drop of 260 feet. It opened just in time for the Northwest Ski Meet and the Central United States Ski Tournament. Spacious grounds around the slide accommodated thirty thousand spectators as well as a network of five- to twelve-mile cross-country skiing courses. St. Paul ski jumpers with national ambitions made do with the Mounds Park slide until the WPA funded a mammoth steel scaffold at Battle Creek in 1939, by which time their city's winter carnivals were once more up and running.[24]

Among the more bizarre winter sports occurrences of the 1930s was the installation of indoor ski slides in each of the Twin Cities' municipal auditoriums. The first Minneapolis slide, erected for the Sportsmen's Show in 1933, was 90 feet high and 250 feet long. Slide and runway were covered with straw to ensure a fast surface, and a canvas strip was placed across the projected end of the course to slow the jumpers down. Anders Haugen, designer of the slide, and his two brothers agreed to give the indoor jump its premier test. Unfortunately, the first jump exceeded the projected distance by twenty-five feet, propelling the skier over the canvas strip and nearly to his death. After readjusting the sliding surface, the two remaining brothers carried on with the show. Haugen followed suit in St. Paul with a longer but less steep slide completed in time for the Sportsmen's Show held in that city in 1937. This time, Anders and his brother Lars thoroughly tested the slide before making a public run.[25]

The annual Sportsmen's Show, held in early November, did not compete directly with outdoor winter sporting events, but other expositions plainly did. From the late 1920s through the brutal winters of the mid-1930s, indoor merchandising shows pulled in the huge winter crowds that had once assembled to march the streets and cavort about the winter castles.

Foremost among these were the great automobile expositions. It is doubtful whether a full-blown winter carnival could have competed. Supported by the advertising dollars of the major car companies and numerous local dealerships, the indoor auto exhibits drew media attention rivaling that of the prewar winter carnival parades.

The closest either city came to hosting multiple-sport events in these years was at Fort Snelling, where tracts of long-unused land in and about the old fort were turned over to ski-joring, coasting, and numerous other snow and ice activities, all informally held, scantily publicized, and nearly bereft of spectators. Bevies of school children slid down the hills and transformed the parade ground of the old fort into an enormous winter playground.

Finally, in 1937, the winter spectacles returned to St. Paul with all of their former pomp and splendor. A vast ice castle in the familiar Central Park setting hazily recalled the medieval themes of the first ice palaces, but its walls bumped in and out, up and down, in the restless fashion of the Zig-Zag Moderne style. Lit from within by varicolored electric bulbs, the translucent structure was said to "blaze with iridescent beauty." The city supplied its own architect, Charles Bassford, for the project. Clarence Wiggington, Bassford's chief assistant, was the probable designer. This arrangement continued through the next five years of ice palace construction.[26]

Zero temperatures and a relentless north wind failed to keep three hundred thousand spectators from jamming the parade route during the first grand pro-

Olympic skier and Minneapolis resident Anders Haugen in 1934. Haugen and his two brothers put on indoor ski-jumping exhibitions at the height of the Great Depression.

Hot water poured onto blocks to cement them at the 1937 St. Paul Winter Carnival. Below-zero temperatures required a boiler on the castle site, so that the water would not freeze before it could be poured from the buckets

cession on Saturday evening, January 30. More than ten thousand spectators assembled at the intersection of Fifth and Robert Street alone, hanging from street lamps, standing on street cars and automobiles, and packing the entire area. By the time the parade finally reached City Hall, four hours late, the mayor's teeth chattered so badly he could scarcely talk.[27]

Forty gigantic rubber balloons in the form of animals highlighted the parade. Shipped in from Philadelphia, they came out again on Monday, when the city's school children were released early for a much more orderly Kiddie Parade. On the following evening, a small detachment of seven marching units carried the pageant into the arena of the municipal auditorium, where Rudi Vallee and His Connecticut Yankees waited. The famed crooner and radio personality promised to "give 'em all the march music they want — and the way they like it for as long as they want it."

Vallee's presence at the 1937 carnival put news of its activities on the nation's air waves. His nightly shows also assured carnival organizers of at least one sort of success whatever the north wind blew in. The orchestra performed a stage revue on opening night, a medley of college songs for a large university crowd, and a program of marches when the parade came through. After his second performance, the *Pioneer Press*, which cosponsored his shows, dubbed Vallee the Crown Prince of the Carnival.[28]

As with previous sports weeks, skating at the hippodrome and ski jumping on the Mounds Park slide dominated the sports schedule. During the 1937 carnival the city hosted the finals of the North American Indoor Skating Championships, where three national records fell. Carnival activities spilled out into other venues as well. Cross-country ski races were held on the Highland Park golf course, broomball contests occurred at the St. Clair playgrounds, and the tobogganing slide went up at its usual location next to the ice castle. The scattering of sporting venues across the city expanded on a tendency toward decentralization of the prewar carnivals and already fully developed in the Iron Range frolics of the mid-1930s.[29]

To stimulate snow-modeling activity and arouse interest in the carnival as a whole, the organizers hired itinerant Bavarian sculptor Joseph Eldbauer to carve several elaborate sculptures out of ice. Eldbauer chose a literary theme, Ben-Hur and his chariot, for

Ski-joring on the Fort Snelling grounds in 1935

his major opus and more wintry themes for lesser pieces. All were located in Rice Park in front of the old federal courthouse, which proved to be a popular venue for artistic ventures at later winter carnivals.

Carnival organizers beat a partial retreat in 1938 by paring the ice palace back to an ice court and moving it to Mounds Park playground on the East Side. A grand stairway flanked by stepped piers swept up to a great half-disc of ice, with an even larger one affixed to the rear. The vast open area in front of the stairs was flooded to form an ice rink. Even more than the ice castle of the year before, the design of the ice court mimicked the bold geometries of the Art Deco style. Moving the castle to the East Side brought skating and skiing, the great exhibition sports of the carnival, into proximity with the usual pageantry surrounding Boreas, the Fire King, and their entourages.

Snow modeling moved to the old city hall square near the southern edge of downtown and this time attracted a number of local talents.

Below-zero temperatures once again greeted the opening parade, but this time city authorities were at least prepared to handle the crush of people. Two hundred fifty uniformed policemen reinforced by 150 fire department volunteers lined the parade route, while the commissioner of public safety flew overhead to radio locations of traffic problems to a police dispatcher. Twenty-five thousand marchers and an imaginative assembly of floats, from knockoffs of Disney movies to glorifications of winter rail travel, braved the cold to create what one reporter described as "St. Paul's greatest parade in two decades of winter carnival history" — a safe claim, since its only competition after 1918 was the fiasco of 1937.[30]

The completed 1937 ice palace, viewed from the quadriga of the State Capitol

Nina Stewart, 1937 carnival queen candidate representing Gokey's

131

The winter of 1939 finally showed what decent weather could do for a Depression-era winter carnival parade. A throng of four hundred thousand spectators, the largest yet assembled in St. Paul for any purpose, witnessed the procession, this time strung out along Summit Avenue as well as downtown. Human flies clung to downtown buildings, the trees of Summit Avenue were alive with onlookers, a hoard of sitters lined the stone walls in front of Summit Avenue mansions, and solid masses of people banked the sloping lawns of the State Capitol and the St. Paul Cathedral. One group even managed to position itself on the State Capitol dome.[31]

Fine weather and weeks of preparation allowed the parade itself to overshadow the theatrical pageantry surrounding King Boreas. For the first time in the century, many parade floats approached the artistic heights and painstaking craftsmanship of those in the

1880s carnivals. As chairman of the parade committee, master furniture designer and craftsman William Yungbauer may have done some prodding. The theme trophy went to the Great Northern Railway, which suspended its usual advertising display in favor of a replica of the 1886 ice palace. Other prizes went to Dayton's Bluff Commercial Club's depiction of the Mounds Park ski slide and a shoe wholesaler's gigantic representation of an ice skate being pulled by a team of penguins, the company's queen candidate nesting in the shoe of the skate.

Outdoor carnival activity in 1939 revolved around three sites: the public land along Kellogg Boulevard, Como Park, and the lower East Side. Ice and snow sculptures pursued numerous themes as they filled nearly all of the public space along Kellogg Boulevard, on the grounds of the old city hall, and in Rice Park. For the first time, the ice castle stood apart from organized sports events. Rising south of the pavilion near the western shore of Lake Como, it was said to be modeled after the storied Arabian Nights castles. Moorish detailing and hundreds of ever-changing

varicolored lights did indeed create the semblance of an oriental fantasy, less remote and lighter in spirit than any of its predecessors. The public flocked to the ice palace, though the only events held in and around

The 1938 ice court with the Crown Prince, Queen of the Snow, King Boreas IV, and the retiring king

The ice court and skating rink in Mounds Park playground, at the 1938 carnival

133

it were the traditional ceremonies involving King Boreas and the Fire King.[32]

The location of King Boreas's throne on Dayton's Bluff had proven to be a one-year experiment, but the East Siders had nothing to complain about. Two mammoth winter sports structures arose in time for the 1939 carnival, and each was located in the vicinity of the 1938 ice court. Late in 1938 the WPA funded construction of a toboggan "super-slide" in Mounds Park and, not far below it, an even more dramatic ski-jumping scaffold and slope in Battle Creek Park. Dubbed Mount Olympus and Mount Pegasus by the carnival association, they drew huge crowds throughout their inaugural season and many winters to follow. The toboggan slope dropped nearly two hundred feet in a run of half a mile, carrying the coasters an additional quarter of a mile on near-level grade. A national ski jumping tournament christened the Battle Creek

The Burlington Railroad float passing before the State Capitol in a 1938 winter carnival parade

The Dayton's Bluff Carnival Club float at the 1939 carnival

slide. Patterned after the famed Garbisch Partenkirchen slide in Bavaria, it was equipped for leaps of 250 feet, well beyond the then-current U.S. record.[33]

Cold weather and the continued rise in popularity of winter sports assured several more years of successive winter carnivals in St. Paul. Each attempted to best the 1939 records in some statistical category or another. The 1940 carnival assembled the world's largest drum and bugle corps, fifteen hundred strong, and also broke (or claimed to have broken) the carnival record for combined number of floats and musical units participating in a parade. A year later, with local participation beginning to taper off, carnival organizers boasted of record numbers of visitors brought in by trains, autos, and airplanes.

In 1942 a season of threateningly warm weather brought theatrical, operatic, and cinematic events in unprecedented numbers under the carnival umbrella.[34]

Farwell, Ozmun, Kirk and Company's float at the 1939 carnival

The Milwaukee Road drum corps and marching unit at the 1939 carnival

At the heart of each festival was the ice palace, which appeared to have found a fixed venue on Lake Como. The 1940 and 1941 versions of the palace, which were practically identical, returned to the medieval imagery of their nineteenth-century forbears. As in the previous years, most of the pageantry associated with the castles occurred after nightfall, allowing their lighting schemes maximum effect. A U.S. Post Office station in the 1940 ice palace

brought in crowds of people during the day to send out letters with its insignia. More crowds flocked into the conservatory, which was fitted with a temporary facade echoing the medieval theme of the palace's architecture. Gothic windows lined one side, and the entry was surmounted by a great circular painting of King Boreas in place of the traditional rose window.

American entry into World War II immediately stilled winter festival activity in the northern cities, but St. Paul managed one last effort. The 1942 carnival pared back most of its outside activities, and much of the remaining festivities were pervaded by a grim military note. A winter with great swings in temperature also dampened enthusiasm. A magnificent palace of three connected pavilions succeeded in reaching a height of only fifteen feet before turning to a mound of slush. Only ski jumping lived up to expectations. Carnival organizers lured so many front-rank skiers to

The ice palace
at Como Park
in 1940

Cypto-Gothic
facade installed
on the Como
Park Conser-
vatory for the
1940 carnival

Cover of the
1942 National
Ski-Jumping
Championships
program in
Duluth

Battle Creek that they could claim with some credibility that the tournament would determine the international champion. A week after that event, Duluth hosted a national championship ski-jumping tournament on its new slide at Fond du Lac, making this a banner year for the sport in Minnesota.[35]

Six straight years of winter carnivals proved that George Thompson's hopes for a sustained carnival tradition in St. Paul were not utterly quixotic. They had simply

been deferred. Winter in the 1890s had proven too mild for ice castle construction and sustained sports activity, as it proved too erratic for completion of the 1942 ice palace. But by 1942, the groundwork was laid for a carnival tradition that only a major international crisis could interrupt. Once that crisis had passed, the St. Paul Winter Carnival returned to stay.

Taking off from
the new Fond du
Lac slide near
Duluth, ca. 1942.
Built in part by
WPA labor,
Duluth's slide
vied with the
Battle Creek
slide in St. Paul.

The program cover reads:

NATIONAL SKI JUMPING CHAMPIONSHIPS

DULUTH
FEBRUARY
7·8·1942

OFFICIAL PROGRAM

AFTERWORD

WINTER CELEBRATIONS TODAY

World War II marked a decisive break in the motivation and spirit of winter celebrations in Minnesota. Combating eastern prejudice about Minnesota weather ceased to be a driving force as population growth plateaued and the state established an industrial and commercial presence as strong as its agricultural roots. St. Paul no longer ached to become another Chicago, or Duluth a Venice of the North. Their growth had peaked, and with stability came a lowered thirst for immigration and speculative investment from outside sources. Promoting mass local participation in outdoor sports also fell by the way as a motivation for organizing winter carnivals. Snow and ice sports had acquired venues and sponsors far more persistent — not to say more prestigious — than anything that winter carnivals had to offer.

What was left from the old carnival mix were pageantry and a handful of exhibition sports. These were the core of the St. Paul Winter Carnival upon its restoration as a "Victory Carnival" in 1946 and for many years thereafter. That first postwar carnival introduced the Ice Capades, an arena show that wove formation skating into Broadway

[facing page]
Skating comic Heine Brock in the Ice Follies of 1945. A three-sport star at the University of Minnesota, the diminutive Brock's rubber-legged antics were a highlight of the Ice Follies for many years.

routines. In 1947, the conversion to indoor spectacle was almost complete, as Boreas's court expanded to encompass 110 Snow Queens and Fire Queens flocking to the carnival from communities around the state. Once again, C. W. Wiggington planned a spectacular ice castle, this time an unabashedly modern monument on Highland Park; once again, it melted into a shapeless mass one third of the way through construction. This was the last ice castle to be attempted for twenty years.

Even the introduction of mutt races in 1952 failed to quell the tide against traditional outdoor activities, as a visit from the Dionne quintuplets captured the eyes of the media. Two years later, the carnival recaptured some of its prewar participation levels with an ice-fishing contest on White Bear Lake. Of all the outdoor sporting events remaining in the carnival, this proved to have the greatest appeal. In 1955 over two thousand fishermen drove out onto the lake, found a spot inside of a 600-foot wheel cleared of snow, punched a hole in the ice, and waited for the catch that would win the fishing-through-the-ice contest.

For the remainder of the 1950s and into the 1960s carnival highlights consisted of a steady stream of television personalities, each of whom presented their shows in the St. Paul Auditorium. Not even the fishing-through-the-ice contest could boast the crowds of Ed Sullivan in 1954, and he was followed by television highlighters Steve Lawrence, Dinah Shore, the "Queen for a Day" show, Jimmy Dean, Howdy Doody, Garry Moore, Steve Allen, Captain Kangaroo, Jim Nabors, and the Smothers Brothers. After the novelty of the White Bear event wore off, only the grand parade and the national speed skating contest on Lake Como offered any sort of outside competition for public attention.[1]

Revival of the winter palace tradition in 1967 signaled the first stage of a gradual awakening from the carnival's fifteen-year bewitchment by television and its stars. Humble though that packed-snow castle was, it once more made winter weather and an outside site the center of festivities. Two years later more than 20,000 children slid out of another snow palace. Yet the television celebrities still lurked about as an insurance policy against the timidity of those thousands for whom winter and carnival had become unwelcome bedfellows.

Recent years have witnessed the erection of two mammoth ice palaces, both erected primarily as showpieces. Their extraordinary price tag — each project cost in excess of $1 million — and their isolation from all but the most closely-guarded carnival activity set them apart from the monuments they were meant to recall and emulate. Rather than serving as a common playground for a diversified and democratic people, they came perilously close to the crystalline extravagances that stupefied the Russian people from a distance on the banks of the Neva.

Insurance regulations forced Ellerbe and Company's centennial design of 1986 to remain closed to the public, and the cramped plan and spiky contours of the design itself inspired passive wonder rather than active engagement. The commercially sponsored ice palace in 1992 was even more devoted

Don Dunlop demonstrating the proper delivery for a curler in 1946

The Scotvold
Twins in the Ice
Follies of 1948

The Scotvold Twins in the Ice Follies of 1948

A. J. Brioschi as a Vulcan in the 1948 St. Paul Winter Carnival

to spectacle without use or context. Designed by Bill Rust and sponsored by a soft-drink manufacturer, it exceeded the height of all previous ice castles. Among its many ice-construction innovations were the carving of blind windows after the blocks were laid up, the fusion of ice blocks with torches, and the pre-assembly of tower caps. Locating the palace on Harriet Island provided an excellent setting for its light show, but it was a monumental piece of ephemeral sculpture and nothing more.[2]

Fortunately for the health and future of the St. Paul Winter Carnival, the high-toned vanity of the last two ice castles failed to hinder the carnival's resurrection during the 1990s as a powerful affirmation of inclusiveness and diversity in the context of a winter celebration. Ice carvings of every style and disposition have become Rice Park fixtures of the carnival, and in their variety and scale they may prove to be a more fitting symbol of what the carnival has come to be than a solitary towering monument . The soul of the carnival has dispersed as it did in the pre–World War I years, into neighborhood games and fêtes, dozens of participatory sports, and a continuous succession of events that flood downtown public spaces and buildings. Such events as oxcart rides, snow rugby, and sleigh rallies have evolved from local oddities into core components of the carnival.

143

simultaneous enjoyment of any other winter pleasure.

In the past decade, however, a spirit of rediscovery and invention has once more invigorated winter carnival planning in many areas of Minnesota. Dogsled racing, after skipping from town to town in the north, has at last settled into Remer and Duluth, hosts of the Mid-Minnesota 150 Sled-Dog Race and the John Beargrease Sled Dog Marathon, respectively. Several other communities include shorter dogsled races in their winter carnivals.

Cross-country skiing races have also risen in popularity, many of them accumulating enough community activity around them to qualify as winter festivals. The grandest among them is the Vasaloppet, an annual affair sponsored by the town and people of Mora. Organized in 1973, it was inspired by a race of the same name — terminating in a town of the same name — in Sweden. On the first weekend in March, up to ten thousand skiers make the 58-kilometer trek over frozen fields and lakes. At the other end of the spectrum is the Freeze Yer Gizzard Blizzard Run, a 10-kilometer race held since 1981 in International Falls, just south of the Canadian border. Now the centerpiece of a ten-day festival appropriately called Icebox Days, the race has inspired a number of colorful ancillary activities, such as "smoosh" races on two-by-fours and candlelight skiing in Voyageurs National Park.

Ice fishing as a celebratory winter activity received a shot in the arm in 1980, with the organization of the Eelpout Festival in Walker. In promoting a fish that is as ugly as it is obscure, the festival has spawned a wealth of lore rivaling that of Paul Bunyan. Said to represent a branch of evolution that was terminated through sheer repulsiveness, the eelpout is reported to migrate annually up roadside drainage ditches from

Outstate winter festivals have had their Dark Ages as well, but from different causes than the media fixation that captured St. Paul after the war. For nearly three decades, ice-fishing contests and snowmobile runs swallowed all other forms of organized winter festivity. The large crowds once gathered at the foot of monumental ski jumps dispersed into villages of fishing houses. Through much of the state, motorized snow craft, once a curiosity, have come to enjoy more miles of trails than the automobile has paved roads. Popular though these two winter diversions are, it would be a pity indeed were the festival spirit statewide to dwindle to a fixation on them alone, one so sluggish as scarcely to pass as a sport and the other so demanding on the environment as to discourage the

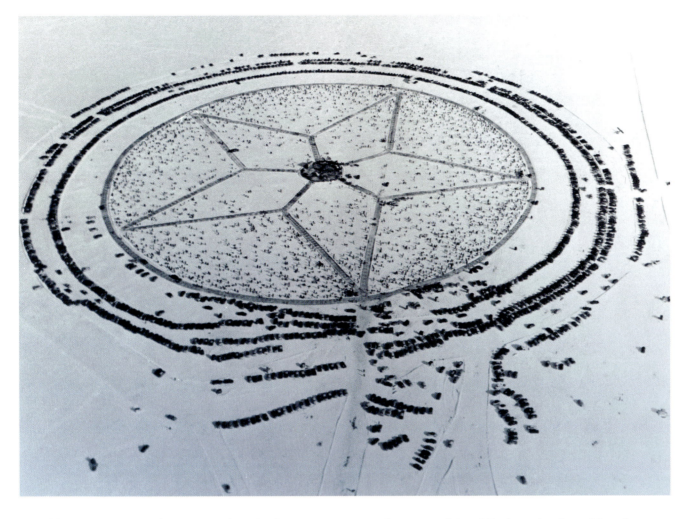

Brooklyn Center, a north Minneapolis suburb, to Leech Lake, the site of the festival. Each year the local paper publishes a special Eelpout Festival edition, which offers co-founder Ken Bresley and his allies the constant opportunity to rewrite the history of the festival, invent new sporting uses of its finned hero (such as 'pout golf and 'pout bowling), and denigrate such local "trash fish" as the walleyed pike and the muskellunge.[3]

All in all, the enormous popularity the Eelpout Festival has achieved probably has as much to do with its promulgation by a breed of journalism recalling the literary excesses of the late nineteenth century as it has to do with the drawing power of the festival events themselves. Festival organizers have capitalized

on the sense of the ridiculous that has seldom been far from successful winter carnivals. It undercuts social conventions, breaks down barriers between strangers, and makes it possible to embrace the most chilling conditions with high spirits. Any living celebration of Minnesota winters requires the same good humor, blissful ignorance of discomfort, and optimistic assessment of the bleakest of conditions that drove Goodhue to rhapsodize about the territory before it became a state.

Just as the Eelpout Festival epitomizes the self-mocking aspect of Minnesota's winter carnival tradition, the Voyageur Winter Festival in Ely captures its highest social and cultural ideals. Established in 1994 as an outgrowth of an annual cross-country ski race,

Part of the snow sculpture garden of the 1987 centennial winter carnival. Japanese snow carvers from Sapporo, Japan, were featured artists at the carnival.

Jeanne Melby winning the 1994 pout-kissing contest at the 1994 Eelpout Festival in Walker

the Ely event pulls together French voyageur pastimes, traditional Ojibway communal activities, earlier carnival sports such as ski-joring and kids' sled-dog races, numerous skiing and snowmobile activities, the educational resources of the local International Wolf Center, and evenings of story-telling by such local luminaries as Ely's most famous sons, arctic explorers Will Steger and Paul Schurke.

As if this weren't enough to entertain all ages, the Voyageur Winter Festival also sponsors a snow sculp-

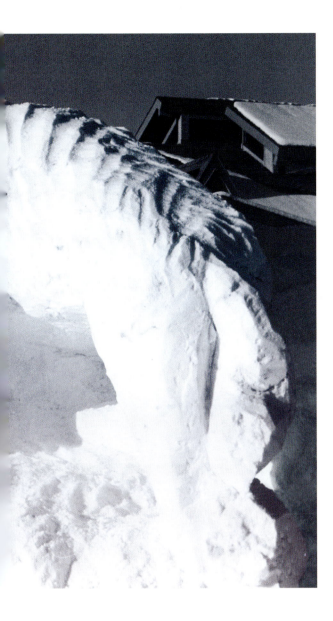

ture symposium, which draws on the increasing number of artists who are becoming proficient in that ephemeral medium, in Japan and Europe as well as North America. Snow and ice sculpting also add a quiet diversion from snowmobiling at the Iron Trail Festival of Lights on the Iron Range and the Nisswa Winter Pageant north of Brainerd.

A number of towns have built lesser winter celebrations around a signature event. Chisholm Polar Bear days sponsors a dog weight pull, in which con-

testants have towed as much as 2300 pounds on a sled. At the Northwest Angle Winterfest, held at the northernmost point on the United States, numerous vehicular races and excursions utilize winter airstrips, ancient fur-trapping trails, and a modern snowmobile trail system that binds communities together over an otherwise trackless frozen wilderness. The snowmobile is joined by giant track vehicles and a Canadian invention, the power toboggan. On a quieter front, the Iron Range town of Tower hosts what it calls a Finlander bocce ball tournament during its Long John Days. The featured event is a peculiar cross between curling and traditional bocce ball. A slab of wood with a handle is the primary piece of equipment.

These are but a sample of the scores of Minnesota winter fêtes that have arisen in recent years. Without exception their reason for being is to keep a northern community alive and open during the long winter months, both for the mental well-being of its townspeople and for the financial health of its businesses. The most successful among them have also attracted visitors and money from well outside their normal commercial reach. But even the smallest and most ephemeral among them testifies to the continued resourcefulness of Minnesotans in discovering and promoting ways to celebrate out-of-doors in the midst of a long and arduous winter.

NOTES

MHS   Minnesota Historical Society
SPMPP *St. Paul and Minneapolis Pioneer Press*
SPPP   *St. Paul Pioneer Press*

I NEVER KNEW (pp. 12–19)

[1] Letter to Jarvis's family, Jan. 2, 1834, the New York Academy of Medicine Library, cited in Peg Meier, *Too Hot, Went to Lake: Seasonal Photos from Minnesota's Past* (Minneapolis: Neighbors Publishing, 1993), 221.

[2] *We Made It Through the Winter: A Memoir of a Northern Minnesota Boyhood* (St. Paul: Minnesota Historical Society Press, 1974), 50

[3] Return I. Holcombe et al, *Minnesota in Three Centuries* (Publishing Society of Minnesota: Mankato, 1908), 2: 63–65.

[4] "The Breaking Up of a Hard Winter," *Minnesota Pioneer*, Apr. 28, 1849.

[5] Isaac Atwater, *History of the City of Minneapolis, Minnesota* (New York: Munsell & Co., 1893), 66.

[6] "An Extraordinary Winter," *SPMPP*, Mar. 21, 1881.

[7] "A Memorable Day," *St. Paul Pioneer*, Jan. 9, 1873.

[8] "The Great Storm, " *Mankato Weekly Review*, Jan. 14, 1873; "The Late Storm: Horrors Developing," *St. Paul Pioneer*, Jan. 11, 1873.

[9] These are figures for the Twin Cities, cited in "An Extraordinary Winter, " *SPMPP*, Mar. 21, 1881. The writer claimed the cumulative snowfall to have been less in the north and greater in the southern and southwestern parts of the state, where the October storm was fiercest.

[10] "No More Snow Blockades," *SPMPP*, Jan. 26, 1888. An interesting piece of evidence for the lack of dramatic late winter storms in the years between 1889 and 1909 is the paucity of rotary plow photographs in Minnesota public collections prior to 1909. The Northern Pacific Railway installed the device on several of its trains in the winter of 1887–88, and the other northwestern lines followed suit the next winter.

THE HEALTHIEST REGION (pp. 20–25)

[1] Untitled flier filed under Dorr and Cummings's name in the Minnesota Historical Society.

[2] "St. Paul," *Minnesota Pioneer*, Apr. 28, 1849. Goodhue, like many of the journalists of his day, took on the mantel of town and territorial moralist as well as promoter. See W. W. Folwell, *A History of Minnesota*, (St. Paul: Minnesota Historical Society, 1956), 1: 251, and Edward D. Neill, "Obituary of James M. Goodhue," *Collections of the Minnesota Historical Society* (St. Paul: Minnesota Historical Society, 1902),1: 245–49.

[3] "The Breaking Up of a Hard Winter," *Minnesota Pioneer*, Apr. 28, 1849. As the column is headed with the words "For the Pioneer," it may not have been written by Goodhue himself.

[4] "To Farmers of the United States and Europe," *Minnesota Pioneer*, Sept. 26, 1850.

[5] "The Weather," *Minnesota Pioneer*, Jan. 2, 1850.

[6] *The Immigrant's Guide to Minnesota in 1856* (St. Anthony: W. W. Wales, 1856), 17–19. J. L. Scripps's comments are on p. 106 and 111.

[7] H. C. Rogers, "General Summary," in *Minnesota as a Home For Immigrants, Being the First and Second Prized Essays Awarded by the Board of Examiners* (St. Paul: Pioneer Press Co., 1866), 84.

[8] Girart Hewitt, *Minnesota: Its Advantages to Settlers* (St. Paul: Privately printed, 1867), 31, 34. Bushnell's tale, written in a letter, first achieved wide circulation in an essay by Mary J. Colburn published in *Minnesota as a Home For Immigrants*, 26. For a longer but largely anecdotal account of Minnesota's health-based boosterism in the 1860s and 1870s, see Helen Clapesattle's "When Minnesota was Florida's Rival," *Minnesota History* 35 (Mar. 1957), 214–21.

[9] Ledyard Bill, *Minnesota; Its Character and Climate* (New York: Wood and Holbrook, 1871), 71–72, 78. The son of a wealthy farmer in New York, Bill's career in regional boost-

erism began at his birth, for he was named after a newly established town. He preceded the Minnesota book with a treatise of similar character on Florida, restricting his praise of that state's healthful conditions, however, to its winter months.

[10] "Minnesota: Its Climate," *Northwestern Tourist*, Oct. 3, 1885.

[11] Henry A. Castle, *Minnesota: Its Story and Biography* (Chicago: Lewis Publishing Co., 1915), 30. Castle's stalwart faith in the unlimited healing powers of Minnesota's climate began with his own recovery from a debilitating illness after moving from Quincy, Illinois, to Minnesota in 1866. See Clapesattle, "When Minnesota Was Florida's Rival."

[12] John P. Owens, "A Winter's Journey to Minnesota in 1852," originally published in the *St. Paul Weekly Minnesotan*, Dec. 11, 1852, reprinted in *Minnesota History* 40 (Winter 1967): 387-90.

[13] Colburn, *Minnesota as a Home For Immigrants*, 20.

[14] "Is This the Frigid Zone?" *SPMPP*, Dec. 3, 1885.

[15] "Minnesota Winter," *Northwest Illustrated Monthly Magazine* 6 (Feb. 1888).

INAUGURATING THE CARNIVAL SEASON (pp. 26-38)

[1] *Minnesota: Its Character and Climate*, 74.

[2] "Life in the Northwest — Society, &c.," *Minnesota Chronicle and Register*, Dec. 22, 1849.

[3] "Minnesota Winter," *Northwest Illustrated Monthly Magazine* 6 (Feb. 1888).

[4] Furness's recollections were written in 1934 and published in "Childhood Recollections of Old St. Paul," *Minnesota History* 29 (June 1948): 116; "Life in the Northwest — Society, &c.," *Minnesota Chronicle and Register*, Dec. 22, 1849; *St. Peter Courier*, Dec. 17, 1856.

[5] The description of the horse-drawn train is taken from a note in *Minnesota Pioneer*, Feb. 27, 1850; that of the dog-train comes from "A Red River Train," *Minnesota Chronicle and Register*, Mar. 2, 1850.

[6] For a similar description of northern Indian toboggan construction and use, see "Fire and Water: Toboggans and Tobogganing," *Minneapolis Tribune*, Jan. 31, 1886. A St. Paul reporter claimed the device to have been constructed of birch bark; see "Tobogganing," *SPMPP*, Winter Carnival Edition, Jan. 30, 1886.

[7] *Minnesota Pioneer*, Mar. 6, 1850.

[8] *SPMPP*, Dec. 18, 1885; "His Idols Broken," *SPMPP*, Dec. 20, 1885.

[9] *Minneapolis Tribune*, Mar. 2, 1885; "Tobogganing in New Jersey," *Frank Leslie's Illustrated Newspaper* 61 (Jan. 23, 1886), 379. The Florence to which the Minneapolis newspaper report refers could also have been an isolated hamlet of that name in upstate New York or even an obscure farming community in southwestern Minnesota, but the Wisconsin locale is much more likely than either of these because of its proximity to an area already established as a summer resort — as was the case with Saratoga, New York.

[10] "The Glittering Castle: Carnival Notes," *SPMPP*, Jan. 11, 1886, "Tobogganing: An Ancient Institution," *SPMPP*, Winter Carnival Edition, Jan. 30, 1886.

[11] *Red Wing Advance Sun*, Jan. 19, 1887; "In a Blaze of Glory: Carnival Pointers," *SPMPP*, Feb. 2, 1886.

[12] "Tobogganing Almost a Sin," *SPMPP*, Jan. 3, 1886. Much of the moral controversy about tobogganing was not reported locally until the sport became a local fad late in 1885.

[13] "Formation of the Parade," *SPMPP*, Jan. 31, 1886; "Defending the Toboggan," *Minneapolis Tribune*, Feb. 8, 1886.

[14] "Tobogganing at Tuxedo," *SPMPP*, Jan. 16, 1887.

[15] Quoted in *Duluth Tribune*, Jan. 23, 1886.

[16] Frank G. O'Brien, "Skating Pleasures of Early Days," in *Minnesota Pioneer Sketches* (Minneapolis: Housekeeper Press, 1904), 236-38. For an excellent account of both the social and the technological aspects of the 1860s skating craze, see Luna Lambert, *The American Skating Mania: Ice Skating in the Nineteenth Century* (Washington, D.C.: National Museum of History and Technology, Smithsonian Institution, 1978).

[17] Six lines in the *St. Paul Globe*, Feb. 8, 1885.

[18] *SPMPP*, Dec. 26, 1885.

[19] G. C. Torguson, "Skiing in Pope County," *Glenwood Herald*, June 12, 1930; G. C. Torguson, "Skiing Then and Now," WPA History Project, ca.1939, unpaginated typed manuscript, Pope County Historical Society, Glenwood.

[20] Torguson, WPA History Project.

[21] Alfred Söderström, *Minneapolis Minnen: Kulturhistorisk Axplockning* (Privately published, 1899), 394-95; "Local Ski Fans Recall Days of Real Sport in Minneapolis," *Minneapolis Tribune*, Jan. 21, 1923.

[22] Carl G. O. Hanson, "First Ski Meet Here Before 1888," *Minneapolis Tribune*, Jan. 1, 1950; "Local Ski Fans"; Kenneth Bjork, *Saga in Steel and Concrete: Norwegian Engineers in America* (Northfield, Minn.: Norwegian-American Historical Association, 1947), 436-37. Bjork's

chronicle of the early days of the Minneapolis Ski Club, like the anonymous1923 *Minneapolis Tribune* article, consists largely of quotations from an account prepared by Illstrup that was then (1947) in the hands of Mrs. Walter Fuchs of Douglas, Minnesota. Söderström credits Ilstrup with establishing the first skiing association in the country ("i hela America") and introducing Americans to skiers of Hemmestvedt's rank but stops short of declaring the 1885 competition the first in this country; Söderström, *Minneapolis Minnen*, 395. Other clubs claiming to have held competitions before the famed 1888 meet at Ishpeming are the Aurora Club of Red Wing, Minnesota, and the Dovre Ski Club of Eau Claire, Wisconsin.

23 "Snow-Shoe Race," *Minneapolis Tribune*, Feb. 23, 1885; *Minneapolis Tribune*, Feb. 24, 1885.

24 *Minneapolis Tribune*, Feb. 24, 1885; "Local Ski Fans Recall Days of Real Sport in Minneapolis," *Minneapolis Tribune*, Jan. 21, 1923. A venue on railroad land may have been chosen to make it easier for skiers from other locations to participate. But the Twin Cities was simply not yet prepared to embrace the sport.

25 "First Club in America Organized Here in 1883" and "Minutes of First Meeting of Aurora Ski Club Found," *Red Wing Daily Eagle*, Feb. 2, 1928. For many years the Aurora Ski Club repeated the claim of this first headline, although the second article clearly dated the organization of the club to a meeting on Jan. 19, 1886. All that happened in 1883 was the attempt to lure Norwegian skiing champions to the area. According to a chronological listing of record jumps compiled by Harold Grinden of Duluth, who was then (1939) historian for the National Ski Association of America, T. (Torjus?) Hemmestvedt held the 1879 record of 74 feet, set at Husbybakken, Norway; recorded by G. C. Torguson, "Skiing Then and Now."

26 Robert G. Dunbar, "Curling and Eveleth," *Missabe Iron Ranger*, Dec. 1952, p. 18. Ronald J. Newell, *Where the Winding Maple Flows* (Privately published, 1978), 103; "Birthplace of Minnesota Curling," *St. Paul Sunday Pioneer Press*, Picture Magazine, Mar. 9, 1969.

27 "The Caledonian Club," *Minneapolis Tribune*, Feb. 7, 1885.

28 *Minnesota Pioneer*, Jan. 16, 1850; Catharine Goddard letter to her sister Lucretia, Dec. 30, 1852, Orrin F. Smith and Family Papers, MHS.

29 "They Went A-Fishing," *Northwestern Tourist*, Feb. 20, 1886.

SOCIETY OVERFLOWS
(pp. 40-61)

1 Russian ice castle stories were endlessly reiterated before and during the first winter carnival. See, for example, the first official publication of the St. Paul Ice Palace and Winter Carnival Association, *St. Paul Ice Palace and Winter Carnival Souvenir*, by J. H. Hanson (St. Paul Ice Palace and Winter Carnival Association, 1885); and "St. Paul Ice Palace and Winter Carnival: The Ice Palace," *Minneapolis Tribune*, Jan. 3, 1886. Most of the local references to Russian ice palaces erroneously ascribe a date of 1741 to Empress Anna's palace and omit mention of an earlier one in 1734. For a much fuller account that draws on authoritative sources, see *Ice Palaces*, by Fred Anderes and Ann Agranoff (New York: Abbeville Press, 1983), 11-15.

2 Peter the Great's cruel invention was chronicled in "The Crystal Palace," *Wilton Weekly News*, Jan. 3, 1867. The product of the French historian Leveque, the legend was presumably picked up by other papers as well. The story of the Empress Anna's ice palace has been retold in modern times by Fred Anderes and Ann Agranoff in *Ice Palaces* (Abbeville Press: New York, 1983), 11-13.

3 At the laying of the cornerstone for the first St. Paul ice palace, Mayor Edmund Rice declared that the proposition to erect it was aided by "young men and middle age, engrossed in business, merchant, mechanic and laborer" and "involves no question of sex, creed or politics" in "Splendid Overture: Mayor Rice's Remarks," *SPMPP*, Jan. 15, 1886.

4 "A New View of the Ice Palace," *SPMPP*, Jan. 8, 1886.

5 "A Winter Carnival," *St. Paul Dispatch*, Oct. 14, 1885; "A Winter Carnival in St. Paul," *St. Paul Dispatch*, Oct. 21, 1885.

6 The remark was made in a speech by Col. Fairman; see "Rivalry as a Potent Factor of Growth," *St. Paul Dispatch*, Oct. 13, 1888.

7 "Rivalry as a Potent Factor of Growth"; untitled editorial remark, *St. Paul Dispatch*, Oct. 22, 1885; "Our Ice Palace Abroad," *St. Paul Dispatch*, Oct. 27, 1885.

8 "In the Chamber: The Matter Considered There," *St. Paul Dispatch*, Nov. 2, 1885; "A Nice Carnival," *St. Paul Dispatch*, Nov. 2, 1885; "Arranging for the Carnival," *SPMPP*, Nov. 15, 1885; and "Grandest on Earth: The Carnival Association," *SPMPP*, Winter Carnival Edition, Jan. 30, 1886; "St. Paul to Have an Ice Palace," *American Architect and Building News*, Nov. 28, 1885.

9 "Successful Carnival," *St. Paul Globe*, Jan. 30, 1885; *Minneapolis Tribune*, Jan. 3, 1886. A newspaper editor in St. Cloud, a city northwest of Minneapolis, anticipated the

criticism, but not the solution, for St. Paul's ice palace fixation. "You attempted to change the sunny clime of Minnesota into a cold Canadian winter, and you have failed — ignominiously failed. It will now go thundering down the ages that ice palaces never can be raised on Minnesota soil," *St. Cloud Times*, quoted in *SPMPP*, Jan. 1, 1886.

[10] *SPMPP*, Dec. 29, 1885, Jan. 1, 1886.

[11] "A New View of the Ice Palace," *SPMPP*, Jan. 8, 1886.

[12] "The Grandest on Earth," *SPMPP*, Winter Carnival Edition, Jan. 30, 1886.

[13] "The New Snow Shoe Club," *SPMPP*, Nov. 18, 1885.

[14] "Grandest on Earth: A Brilliant Spectacle," *SPMPP*, Winter Carnival Edition, Jan. 30, 1886.

[15] "Season of Winter Sports," *SPMPP*, Nov. 16, 1885; "Curling, Past and Present," *SPMPP*, Jan. 30, 1886.

[16] "The Coming Carnival," *SPMPP*, Dec. 8, 1885. While reporting ski club disgruntlement over the persistent mispronunciation of their equipment, the *Pioneer Press* came up with the strange hybrid "Ski Snowshoe club"; see "Will Be Done on Time: Carnival Notes," *SPMPP*, Jan. 26, 1886.

[17] Anderes and Agranoff, *Ice Palaces*, 25; "The St. Paul Ice Castle and Carnival," *Frank Leslie's Illustrated Newspaper* 61 (Jan. 16, 1886). After an initial reference to the Messrs. Hutchinson, the local press appeared to forget that there were two of them, referring to each as he came to town (apparently they never came together) as if he alone were the architect.

[18] "Perfecting the Plans," *SPMPP*, Dec. 2, 1885; "The Coming Carnival," *SPMPP*, Dec. 8, 1885.

[19] "The Ice Palace as It Will Appear," *SPMPP*, Dec. 3, 1885.

[20] These measurements are given in the initial publication of the plans in "The Ice Palace as It Will Appear," *SPMPP*, Dec. 3, 1885, and repeated in later newspaper reports. The size grew with age. According to the *American Architect and Building News*, Dec. 11, 1886, the maximum dimensions were 154 by 180 feet, while in "Our Winter Festival," *Northwest Illustrated Monthly Magazine* (Feb. 1888), they were reported to be 160 by 180 feet.

[21] *SPMPP*, Winter Carnival Edition, Jan. 30, 1886; "The Carnival: News and Notes," *SPMPP*, Jan. 8, "Cold Wave and Carnival," *SPMPP*, Jan. 11, "The Glittering Castle," *SPMPP*, Jan. 13, and "It Is Growing Rapidly, *SPMPP*, Jan. 18, all 1886

[22] "The Glittering Castle," *SPMPP*, Jan. 13, 1886; "The St. Paul Ice Palace," *Harper's Weekly*, Feb. 20, 1886, p. 119.

[23] "The Ice Carnival Booms," *SPMPP*, Jan 12, 1886; "To Lay the Corner Block: News and Notes," *SPMPP*, Jan 14, 1886; "The Carnival Draws Near: Carnival Notes,"

SPMPP, Jan. 22, 1886; "Will Be Done on Time: Carnival Notes," *SPMPP*, Jan. 26, 1886; "Everybody Enthusiastic: Carnival Notes," *SPMPP*, Jan. 27, 1886; "The Three Excursions: Carnival Notes," *SPMPP*, Jan. 28, 1886. The dimensions of the Ortonville block suggest that it was raised by the massive hoists at the granite quarry; it would have had to have been cut down prior to shipment, for neither its bulk nor its weight (ca. 28 tons) could have been handled by block and tackle at the railroad yard. Glencoe, Minnesota, and Big Stone and Bismarck, Dakota Territory, also contributed blocks of unrecorded dimension. A summary report gave the Wahpeton block size as eight by five by two feet, making it the probable monster of the group; "The Carnival at Hand," *SPMPP*, Jan. 29, 1886.

[24] "Bouncing of the Boys," *SPMPP*, Winter Carnival Edition, Jan. 30, 1886; "The Jolly Snowshoers," *Duluth Tribune*, Feb. 9, 1886.

[25] "A Cold Game of Curling," *SPMPP*, Jan. 23, 1886; "The Ice Carnival Booms," *SPMPP*, Jan. 12, 1886; "The Ice Bear Club," *SPMPP*, Winter Carnival Edition, Jan. 30, 1886.

[26] "It Is Growing Rapidly," *SPMPP*, Jan. 18, 1886.

[27] "A Splendid Overture: The Clubs Have Sport," *SPMPP*, Jan. 15, 1886.

[28] "The Three Excursions: Carnival Notes," *SPMPP*, Jan. 28, 1886.

[29] "A Splendid Overture: Laying the Corner Blocks," *SPMPP*, Jan. 15, 1886.

[30] "Everybody Enthusiastic," *SPMPP*, Jan. 10, 1886; "On the Carnival Grounds," *SPMPP*, Jan. 7, 1886; "Painting Red Wing Red: Carnival Notes," *SPMPP*, Jan. 20, 1886.

[31] *Minneapolis Tribune*, Jan. 3, 1886; "Welcome the Veterans: Carnival Notes," *SPMPP*, Feb. 12, 1886; "St. Paul Ice Castle and Carnival," *Frank Leslie's Illustrated Newspaper*, Jan. 16, 1877; "St. Paul's Ice Carnival," *Frank Leslie's Illustrated Newspaper*, Feb. 13, 1886; *Harper's Weekly*, Feb 20, 1886.

[32] "Fire and Water," *Minneapolis Tribune*, Jan. 31, 1886.

[33] "A Storm at Stillwater," *SPMPP*, Jan. 16, 1886; "Painting Red Wing Red," *SPMPP*, Jan. 20, 1886; "Stillwater News," *SPMPP*, Jan. 23, 1886.

[34] "The Excursions," *SPMPP*, Jan. 21, 1886; "A Cold Game of Curling: Grand Army Day," *SPMPP*, Jan. 23, 1886; "Faribault Disappointed," *SPMPP*, Jan. 24, 1886; "The Three Excursions," *SPMPP*, Jan. 28, 1886; "Stillwater News," *SPMPP*, Jan. 23, 1886.

[35] "A Cold Game of Curling: Carnival Notes," *SPMPP*, Jan. 23, 1886; "The Three Excursions," *SPMPP*, Jan. 28, 1886; "Carnival Fragments," *SPMPP*, Feb. 4, 1886; *Duluth Daily Tribune*, Jan. 9, 1886; "Transpiring in Duluth," *Duluth*

Daily Tribune, Jan. 22, 1886; "Duluth's Snow Clubs," *SPMPP*, Jan. 29, 1886; "Secure Your Tickets," *Duluth Daily Tribune*, Feb. 2, 1886.

[36] "Preparing for the Carnival," *SPMPP*, Dec. 20, 1885; "On the Carnival Grounds," *SPMPP*, Jan. 7, 1886; "A Splendid Overture: The Procession and the Carnival," *SPMPP*, Jan. 15, 1886.

[37] "Everybody Enthusiastic: Carnival Notes," *SPMPP*, Jan. 10, 1886; "To Red Wing Tonight: Carnival Notes," *SPMPP*, Jan. 19, 1886; "Ice Statues," *SPMPP*, Feb. 5, 1886.

[38] "The Carnival at Hand: Carnival Notes," *SPMPP*, Jan. 29, 1886; "Preparing for the Carnival," *SPMPP*, Dec. 20, 1885; "A Storm at Stillwater: The Arches," *SPMPP*, Jan. 17, 1886; "At the Grounds: Grand Arch," *SPMPP*, Feb. 2, 1886.

[39] "The Carnival at Hand: Carnival Notes," *SPMPP*, Jan. 29, 1886; "Will Be Done on Time," *SPMPP*, Jan. 26, 1886; "Announcement and Notes," *SPMPP*, Feb. 1, 1886; "How to Enjoy the Winter: The Crocus Hill Slide," *SPMPP*, Feb. 16, 1886; "Tobogganing in Minneapolis," *SPMPP*, Winter Carnival Edition, Jan. 30, 1886; "The Fun of Sliding," *Minneapolis Tribune*, Jan. 10, 1886.

[40] "In a Blaze of Glory," *SPMPP*, Feb. 2, 1886.

[41] "The Ice Fete Program," *SPMPP*, Jan. 24, 1886; "Now Push, All Together," *SPMPP*, Jan. 25, 1886; "Will Be Done on Time," *SPMPP*, Jan. 26, 1886.

[42] "The Dog Trains: A Queer Way to Travel," *SPMPP*, Feb. 6, 1886; "Wonderful Service of Dogs: A Train from Hudson Bay," *SPMPP*, Feb. 9, 1886.

[43] "Carnival Notes," *SPMPP*, Jan. 24, 1886; "Carnival's First Week: Indians at the Carnival," *SPMPP*, Feb. 7, 1886; "Hail, Cold Weather: Afternoon Gaiety: The Red Man's Parade," *SPMPP*, Feb. 9, 1886

[44] "The King of Caloric: Carnival Notes," *SPMPP*, Feb. 5, 1886; "The Son of the Forest Rejoiceth," *SPMPP*, Feb. 1, 1886.

[45] "Good for the Fun Makers," *SPMPP*, Winter Carnival Edition, Jan. 30, 1886; "The Ice Fete Program: Providing for the People," *SPMPP*, Jan. 24, 1886; "The Three Excursions: Accommodating the Crowd," *SPMPP*, Jan. 28, 1886; "The Crowds in the City," *SPMPP*, Feb. 13, 1886; "To Lay the Corner Block: News and Notes," *SPMPP*, Jan. 14, 1886; "King Carnival's Reign: Announcement and Notes," *SPMPP*, Feb. 1, 1886.

[46] "Fall From the Ice Palace," *Minneapolis Tribune*, Jan. 29, 1886; "The Carnival Not Ended," *SPMPP*, Feb. 14, 1886. The *Pioneer Press* made light of the first injury by blaming it on the victim's carelessness, misspelling his name, and misidentifying him as a Swede, while the Minneapolis paper stuck to the facts and got them right.

[47] "The Carnival to Continue," *SPMPP*, Feb. 15, 1886; "How to Enjoy the Winter," *SPMPP*, Feb. 16, 1886.

[48] "One Year Ago," *SPMPP*, Jan. 16, 1887; "The Carnival Draws Near: The Toboggan Slide," *SPMPP*, Jan. 22, 1886; "The Ice Fete: More Slides Needed," *SPMPP*, Jan. 24, 1886; "Tobogganing," *SPMPP*, Winter Carnival Edition, Jan. 30, 1886; "The Opening Procession: Carnival Notes," *SPMPP*, Jan. 30, 1886.

THE MIRACLE (pp. 62–81)

[1] "The Carnival to Continue: Will It Last?" *SPMPP*, Feb. 15, 1886; "Our Winter Festival," *Northwest Illustrated Monthly Magazine* 6 (Feb. 1888): 1.

[2] "Carnival's First Week: The Lessons," *SPMPP*, Feb. 7, 1886; "All for Sport," *SPMPP*, Jan. 16, 1887.

[3] "Our Winter Festival," *Northwest Illustrated Monthly Magazine* 6 (Feb. 1888): 4.

[4] "The Coming Carnival Time: West St. Paul Association," *SPMPP*, Jan. 1, 1887.

[5] "The Coming Carnival Time: Sports in the Park," *SPMPP*, Jan. 1, 1887; "Curlers at the Carnival: Snowshoes and Skis," *SPMPP*, Jan. 26, 1887.

[6] "The Carnival Clubs," *SPMPP*, Jan. 16, 1887; "A Brilliant Defense: Carnival Echoes," *SPMPP*, Jan. 21, 1887; "Winter's Rare Sports: The Boys from Bozeman," *SPMPP*, Jan. 22, 1887; "Advance Tourists," *Duluth Tribune*, Jan. 21, 1887.

[7] "The Coming Carnival: St. Paul in Full Dress," *SPMPP*, Jan. 1, 1887; "Carnival Time Half Gone: Carnival Small Notes," *SPMPP*, Jan. 23, 1887.

[8] "A Brilliant Defense: Equipage Display," *SPMPP*, Jan. 21, 1887; "The Great Day of Days: The Equipage Display," *SPMPP*, Jan. 28, 1887.

[9] "The Great Day of Days: The Dog Parade," *SPMPP*, Jan. 28, 1887.

[10] "The Coming Carnival Time: The Winter's Sports," *SPMPP*, Jan. 1, 1887; "Carnival Time Half Gone: The Indian Village," *SPMPP*, Jan. 23, 1887.

[11] "Ready For the Carnival: Street of Rare Beauty," *SPMPP*, Jan. 16, 1887; "Carnival Time Half Gone: First Week of the Carnival," *SPMPP*, Jan. 23, 1887; "Ready For the Carnival: 'Twill Be a Blaze of Glory," *SPMPP*, Jan. 16, 1887; "Make It a Memorable Week: Two Carnival Expressions," *SPMPP*, Jan. 24, 1887.

[12] "The Great Day of Days: The Crowd," *SPMPP*, Jan. 28, 1887; "The Carnival Ended," *SPMPP*, Jan. 30, 1887.

[13] "Welcome to the King: The Parade," *SPMPP*, Jan. 26, 1888.

[14] "Borealis' Big Day: Chips from the Ice Palace," *SPMPP*, Feb. 1, 1888; "Glory of the Carnival: Fourth Division," *SPMPP*, Feb. 2, 1888.

[15] "A Miniature Carnival: The Indian Village," *SPMPP*, Jan. 28, 1888; "Borealis' Big Day: The Indian Sham Battle," *SPMPP*, Feb. 1, 1888; "Wedded at the Ice Palace," *SPMPP*, Feb. 2, 1888.

[16] "King Borealis Comes: Cut Out of Ice," *SPMPP*, Jan. 25, 1888; "Borealis' Big Day: Chips from the Ice Palace," *SPMPP*, Feb. 1, 1888; "The Fire King Reigns: Ice Statuary," *SPMPP*, Feb. 3, 1888; "The Last of the Carnival: Prizes for the Young Folks," *SPMPP*, Feb. 5, 1888.

[17] "Borealis' Big Day: Chips from the Ice Palace," *SPMPP*, Feb. 1, 1888; "Glory of the Carnival: The Bonspiel Ended," *SPMPP*, Feb. 2, 1888.

[18] "The 'Carnival City,'" *SPMPP*, Jan. 1, 1889; "St. Paul's Winter Carnival," *Frank Leslie's Illustrated Weekly Newspaper* 65 (Jan. 28, 1888), 398.

[19] *Red Wing Advance Sun*, Feb. 15, 1888.

[20] "The Palace of Ice," *St. Paul Daily Globe*, Dec. 23, 1888.

[21] "On with the Carnival," *SPMPP*, Jan. 19, 1896; "New Ruler of St. Paul: Behold the Queen," *SPMPP*, Jan. 22, 1896.

[22] "Legislators in Mock Session," *SPMPP*, Jan. 23, 1896.

[23] "Opens with Grand Parade," *SPMPP*, Jan. 21, 1896.

[24] "New Ruler of St. Paul: Behold the Queen," *SPMPP*, Jan. 22, 1896.

[25] "Fort Karnival," *SPMPP*, Jan. 22, 1896.

[26] "Indians Arrive," *SPMPP*, Jan. 24, 1896.

[27] "Carnival Clubs Grand Parade," *SPMPP*, Jan. 25, 1896; "Many Curlers Are Coming," *SPMPP*, Jan. 21, 1896.

[28] Alexander Macrae, *Reminiscences of the Curling Game in Duluth* (Privately printed, 1924), 3-5.

[29] "Carnival Programme," *SPMPP*, Jan. 21, 1896; "Almost a Lost Art," *Minneapolis Journal*, Dec. 21, 1900.

[30] "Carnival Programme," *SPMPP*, Jan. 21, 1896; "Amusement for Everybody: Racing Features," *SPMPP*, Jan. 24, 1896; "Carnival Clubs Grand Parade: Ice Events," *SPMPP*, Jan. 25, 1896.

[31] "Residence of Davidson," *SPMPP*, Jan. 25, 1896; "Skating Races Have Begun," *SPMPP*, Jan. 28, 1896. McCulloch's only other listing in *Pioneer Press* program notes was as referee for the curling finals between Winnipeg and Minneapolis.

[32] "The Amateur Championships," *Minneapolis Journal*, Dec. 18, 1899; Rolf Fjelstad, "Skating," typed manuscript in the *Minneapolis Journal* files, ca. 1936, special collections of Minneapolis Public Library.

[33] "The Leadville Ice Palace," *Frank Leslie's Illustrated Weekly Newspaper* 81 (Jan. 2, 1896), 6; "Quebec's Winter Carnival," *Frank Leslie's Illustrated Weekly Newspaper* 81 (Feb. 13, 1896), 11. The Quebec and Leadville ice palaces are illustrated and described in detail by Fred Anderes and Ann Agranoff in *Ice Palaces* (New York: Abbeville Press, 1983), 67-83. Leadville's ice palace was never completed because of a freakishly warm December, but it still exuded more raw power and a greater sense of unity than any of the completed St. Paul ice palaces. One of the first New England winter sports carnivals is described in "The Carnival at Albany," *Frank Leslie's Illustrated Weekly Newspaper* 65 (Jan. 28, 1888), 431. The Albany ice castle, dubbed Fort Orange, was supposed to be a mockup of a structure built by the Dutch on the Albany site. Albany and Essex County, New Jersey, had both hosted coasting carnivals, featuring bobsledding and tobogganing, respectively, the year of St. Paul's first winter carnival. See "Coasting Carnival in Albany," *Frank Leslie's Illustrated Newspaper* 61 (Jan. 30, 1886), 395, and "Tobogganing in New Jersey," *Frank Leslie's Illustrated Newspaper* 61 (Jan. 23, 1886), 379.

THIS WINTER PLAYGROUND (pp. 82-95)

[1] "New-Year Day," *St. Paul Pioneer*, Jan. 3, 1883. The reporter's references to "the Lake" might also mean White Bear Lake.

[2] *Northwestern Tourist*, Dec. 26, 1885; "Icicles," *Northwestern Tourist*, Jan. 9, 1886.

[3] "Fastest of the Ice Boats," *St. Paul Pioneer Press*, Jan. 5, 1896.

[4] "Ice Yacht Race," *Lake City Republican*, Feb. 3, 1894.

[5] "Fastest of the Ice Boats"; "Ice Boat Chat," *Lake City Republican*, Jan. 8, 1898.

[6] Wells Eastman, "The Famous Ice Boat, Northern Light," *Hennepin County History* 23, (Winter 1964), 9-10.

[7] The Hudson River craft proved particularly short-lived, largely because they had been poorly stored for several years before being auctioned off. Ward Burton enjoyed only one season with the *Northern Light*, after which its spine collapsed from dry rot.

[8] *Red Wing Advance Sun*, Feb. 16, 1887.

[9] G.C. Torguson, "Skiing in Pope County," *Glenwood Herald*, June 15, 1930; hand-written notes copied from

Starbuck newspapers in clippings file on skiing, Pope County Historical Society; "Holmenkollen near Glenwood," *Glenwood Herald*, Jan. 12, 1912.

[10] Harold A. Grinden, "The Duluth Ski Club Through Fifty Golden Years," lecture for fiftieth anniversary program [1955], typescript in Northeast Minnesota History Center, Duluth; "Ski Coasting in the Northwest," *Northwest Illustrated Monthly Magazine* 15 (Dec. 1897).

[11] Harold A. Grinden, "The Duluth Ski Club"; G.C. Torguson, "Skiing Then and Now: Ski Hill Record Jumps," WPA History Project, ca.1939.

[12] Harold A. Grinden, "Coleraine Famous for Skiing," *Missabe Iron Ranger*, Dec. 1954, p. 13.

[13] *Fergus Falls Daily Journal*, Feb. 10, 1911.

[14] "Want Ski Tournament in 1912," *Virginia Daily Enterprise*, Feb. 13, 1911.

[15] Rolf Fjelstad, "Skiing," typed manuscript in the *Minneapolis Journal* files, ca. 1936, special collections of Minneapolis Public Library.

[16] Macrae, *Reminiscences*, 5-6; Hank Kehborn, "Curling Began in 1886," *SPPP*, May 11, 1958.

[17] Robert G. Dunbar, "Curling and Eveleth," *Missabi Iron Ranger*, Dec. 1952, p. 18.

[18] S. Skip Farrington, Jr., *Skates, Sticks, and Men: The Story of Amateur Hockey in the United States* (New York: David McKay Co., 1972), 51; *Minnesota Ariel*, Feb. 1895; both cited in David A. Uppgaard, "Minnesota Hockey," 5-6, typescript essay in MHS collections.

[19] *Minnesota Amateur Hockey Association 1980-81/Articles/By-Law/Regulations*, 43, cited in Upgaard, "Minnesota Hockey," 6-7.

[20] Bruce E. Nowlen, "Minnesota Ice Racing," 1-2, type-script essay in the collections of Hennepin County Historical Society; "The Horse Race," *Lake City Republican*, Jan. 8, 1898.

[21] Nowlen, "Minnesota Ice Racing," 2, 13; "Chisholm Nags Take First," *Virginia Daily Enterprise*, Feb. 13, 1911.

[22] "The Coasters," *Duluth News Tribune*, Jan. 14, 1922.

WE WANT (pp. 96-117)

[1] "Cold Wave Bringing Carnival Weather to Hit Here Today," *SPPP*, Jan. 27, 1916; "Thousands Face Wind and Snow to Join in Frolics of Carnival," *SPPP*, Jan. 29, 1916; "St. Paul Wants Men Who Have Time for Play, Hill Declares," *SPPP*, Jan. 30, 1916.

[2] "Northwest Will Come to Carnival with Record Crowds"; *SPPP*, Jan. 25, 1916; "Hill Outdoes Boys on Dayton's Slide," *SPPP*, Jan. 27, 1916; "Thousands Face Wind and Snow to Join in Frolics of Carnival," *SPPP*, Jan. 29, 1916; "Toboggan Slides Thronged," *SPPP*, Jan. 28, 1916; "'No One Can Stop It Now' L. W. Hill Says of Carnival," *SPPP*, Jan. 28, 1916.

[3] "Carnival Marchers Will Be Near 10,000," *SPPP*, Jan. 27, 1916; "No End to Parade, But Spectators Came to Stay," *SPPP*, Jan. 27, 1916; "All St. Paul is Out for Great Parade Opening Carnival," *SPPP*, Jan. 28, 1916. Pre-estimates based on club registration put the figure just under 10,000; a published estimate the following day raised it to 15,000.

[4] "Boreas Rex Unable to Select a Queen," *SPPP*, Jan. 26, 1916; "Barbecue Will Be Suburbs Offering," *SPPP*, Jan. 30, 1916; "Many Events on Program for Carnival Crowd Today," *SPPP*, Jan. 29, 1916; "Add Trap Shooting to Carnival Sports," *SPPP*, Jan. 25, 1916; "Millions Will Enjoy Carnival in Movies," *SPPP*, Jan. 30, 1916.

[5] "Time Is Short for Aspiring Artists," *SPPP*, Jan. 25, 1916; "Art Student Draws Best Carnival Sketch; More Than 700 Compete," *SPPP*, Jan. 30, 1916.

[6] "Northwest Will Come to St. Paul Carnival with Record Crowds," *SPPP*, Jan. 25, 1916; "Big Crowd Out for Pushball at Island," *SPPP*, Jan. 29, 1916; "Carnival Opening Crowded with Unusual Features," *SPPP*, Jan. 27, 1916.

[7] Note on the back of a C. P. Gibson photograph of a decorated automobile in MHS collections.

[8] "De Ronda Does Big Jump, Then Learns Deal Is Off," *SPPP*, Jan. 27, 1916.

[9] "Steer Jumps Into River, Giving Thousands Thrill," *SPPP*, Jan. 30, 1916.

[10] "Carnival Opening Crowded with Unusual Features," *SPPP*, Jan. 27, 1916; "Fame of St. Paul's Winter Carnivals to Spread to World Corners," *SPPP*, Jan. 30, 1916; "Carnival Spirit Is Found Contagious," *SPPP*, Jan. 29, 1916.

[11] "City Is Saturated with Enthusiasm for Outdoor Fete" and "Big Outdoor Fete Benefits Business," *SPPP*, Jan. 21, 1917.

[12] "Babylonians First to Have Carnival; Rome Close Second," *SPPP*, Jan. 21, 1917.

[13] "St. Paul Buried Under Worst Snowstorm in Recent Years," *SPPP*, Jan. 22, 1917; "Festival at Como Sunday to Be Full of Thrilling Races," *SPPP*, Jan. 26, 1917; "Carnival Spirit Loosed in City on Perfect Day," *SPPP*, Jan. 28, 1917.

[14] "75,000 Brave Cold to See Parade of Industrial Floats" and "Fifty Clubs Enter Floats in Parade; Cold King Routed," *SPPP*, Feb. 2, 1917.

[15] "City's Greatest Fete Has Triumphal Close; 1,000 Dance in Street," *SPPP*, Feb. 4, 1917.

[16] *Official Souvenir View Book, St. Paul Outdoor Sports Carnival, Jan. 27-Feb. 3, 1917* [St. Paul: St. Paul Outdoor Sports Carnival Association, 1917]; "Facts in Dog Race; End May Be Tonight," *SPPP*, Feb. 2, 1917; "Hartman, in Semi-Conscious Condition, Finishes Dog Race," *SPPP*, Feb. 2, 1917. Two boys from Sauk Centre volunteered to break the trail for a ways and ended up walking with the team most of the ninety-five miles to St. Paul, going almost two days without sleep in temperatures bottoming out at thirty below zero.

[17] "Albert Campbell, Race Victor, Fulfills Order of Dying Father," *SPPP*, Feb. 4, 1917.

[18] "Hartman, in Semi-Conscious Condition, Finishes Dog Race," "Queen Raising Fund for Fred Hartman," and "Dog Derby Hero Praised in Poem by St. Paul Man," *SPPP*, Feb. 4, 1917.

[19] "Week's Wholesome Fun Brings Call for 1918 Carnival," *SPPP*, Feb. 4, 1917.

[20] Alvin Swanson, *Life in the Northland, 1897-1920* (Privately published, ca. 1920), copy in MHS collections.

[21] *History and Destiny of Eveleth* (Eveleth, Minn.: Eveleth Commercial Club, 1921), 37-39, 42.

[22] For a complete program of the carnival, see "On with the Carnival: Eveleth Home-Coming Carnival Honoring Returned Soldiers, Sailors, and Marines," *Eveleth News*, Jan. 1, 1920.

[23] "Eveleth Carnival Is Most Successful Affair," *Eveleth News*, Jan. 8, 1920.

[24] *History and Destiny of Eveleth*, 41; G. P. Finnegan, "The Eveleth Hockey Story," *Missabi Iron Ranger*, Dec. 1952, p. 16.

[25] "Eveleth Carnival Is Most Successful Affair," *Eveleth News*, Jan. 8, 1920; dated photographs of the three Eveleth School District toboggan slides in MHS collections.

[26] "Publish Events for Big Carnival Here," *Hibbing Daily News*, Jan. 6, 1921; "Foundation Laid for Ice Palace," *Hibbing Daily News*, Feb. 8, 1921; the schedule of events was published daily in the *Hibbing Daily News* on Feb. 11, 12, and 13.

[27] "Greatest Event Staged in the North, Said," *Hibbing Daily News*, Feb.11, 1921; "Forty Skaters to Enter Race," *Hibbing Daily News*, Feb. 8, 1921.

[28] "Official Invitation from Duluth's Frolic Committee to All Firms and Individuals in Duluth," collections of the Northeast Minnesota Historical Center.

[29] "Official Invitation"; "More Than 20,000 in West End Join in Winter Frolic," *Duluth Herald*, Feb. 12, 1926; "Frolic Facts and Frivolities," *Duluth Herald*, Feb. 15, 1926; "Synopsis of Program: Duluth Winter Frolic," [1926], collections of Northeast Minnesota Historical Center.

[30] "First Annual Winter Frolic in Duluth Passes into History," *Duluth Herald*, Feb. 15, 1926; Harold A. Grinden, "The Duluth Ski Club Through Fifty Golden Years," lecture for fiftieth anniversary program [1955], typescript in Northeast Minnesota Historical Center.

[31] "He Made Duluth Frolic Advertising National in Scope and Gets Results," *Duluth Herald*, Feb. 25, 1927.

[32] "Official Program of the Duluth Winter Frolic" [1927] and "Duluth Winter Frolic Official Program," [1928], both in collections of Northeast Minnesota Historical Center; "Winter Frolic Dropped; Sport to Be Fostered," *Duluth News Tribune*, Nov. 28, 1928.

[33] "Winter Frolic Events to Be Auctioned Off to High 'Bidder'; Meet Tonight," *Hibbing Daily News*, Jan. 21, 1926; "Outdoor Fete to Be Sponsored by 100 Local Groups," *Hibbing Daily News*, Jan. 22, 1926; "Winter Fete Tomorrow at the Locations," *Hibbing Daily News*, Feb. 11, 1926; "Champion Speed Artist is Rink Frolic Feature" and "Score of Best Ice Figure Skaters in Northwest to Be at Rink Carnival Sun.," *Hibbing Daily News*, Feb. 13, 1926; "Hibbing Sports Activities Center at Memorial Hall," *Hibbing Daily News*, Feb. 21, 1927; "Locations on Eve of Celebrations to Be Held in Nature of Winter Frolics," *Hibbing Daily Tribune*, Feb. 16, 1928.

[34] "Virginia Carnival of Sport and Gaiety Starts Monday; To Continue Through Week," *Virginia Daily Enterprise*, Feb. 17, 1926; "Race Prizes to Be Attractive," *Virginia Daily Enterprise*, Feb. 20, 1929.

[35] "Skating Ace to Appear in Frolic," *Chisholm Tribune-Herald*, Jan. 20, 1927.

[36] "Aurora Club Host to Kings of Slid," *SPPP*, Jan. 15, 1928.

[37] "Skiers Pour in from All Sections," *Red Wing Daily Eagle*, Feb. 2, 1928; "Red Wing Turns Out in Force to Welcome Ski Riders," *St. Paul Dispatch*, Feb. 3, 1928.

FROLICKING (pp. 118-138)

[1] "Winter Play Period Opens on Thursday," *Duluth Herald*, Feb. 14, 1933; "Cold Weather Week's Rule" and "Weather Has Made Ski Slide Exceptionally Fast for Sunday's Event," *Ely Miner*, Feb. 10, 1933.

[2] "Winter Sports at Work Farm All Day Sunday," *Duluth Herald*, Feb. 10, 1933; "Camp Sigel Winter Sports," *Ely Miner*, Feb. 17, 1933.

[3] "Winter Sports Finals in Rural Area on Sunday," *Duluth Herald*, Feb. 16, 1935; "Frolic Winners to Compete in County Finals Sunday," *Duluth News Tribune*, Feb. 25, 1936.

[4] "American Legion Winter Carnival to Start Today," [Cloquet] *Pine Knot*, Feb. 24, 1933.

[5] "Frolic Feb. 26 at Crane Lake," *Duluth Herald*, Feb. 13, 1933; "Crane Lake," *Ely Miner*, Feb. 3, 1933.

[6] "Ice Carnival Slated at Hipp January 21," *Eveleth News*, Jan. 12, 1933.

[7] "2,000 attend Winter Sports Event at Lake," *Eveleth News*, Feb. 15, 1934.

[8] "Winter Sports Frolic Proves Big Attraction to Thousands at Lake," *Eveleth News*, Feb. 14, 1935; "Winter Sports Frolic Again Set for Sunday," *Eveleth News*, Feb. 27, 1936; "Winter Frolic Attracted Large Crowd Sunday," *Eveleth News*, Mar. 5, 1936.

[9] "Winter Carnival," *Chisholm Tribune-Herald*, Feb. 7, 1935; "Junior Chamber Completes Plans for Big Event," *Chisholm Tribune-Herald*, Feb. 21, 1935; "Winter Fetes Are Attended by Thousands," *Duluth News-Tribune*, Mar. 2, 1936; *Duluth News-Tribune*, Feb. 29, 1936, and Feb. 17, 1937; "Intercity Jaunt Biggest Held On the Iron Range," *Hibbing Daily Tribune*, Feb. 21, 1938.

[10] "12 Communities Stage Frolics," *Hibbing Daily Tribune*, Feb. 19, 1938; notes on back of Laskiainen photographs in the collections of the Iron Range Research and Interpretive Center, Chisholm.

[11] "Intercity Jaunt Biggest Held on the Iron Range," *Hibbing Daily Tribune*, Feb. 21, 1938.

[12] "Plans Completed for Winter Frolic in Chisholm Sunday," [Virginia] *Queen City Sun*, Feb. 17, 1939; "Snow Train Chartered for Frolic," *Duluth Herald*, Feb. 23, 1940.

[13] *Hibbing Daily Tribune*, Feb. 20, 1937; numerous photographs with backnotes in the photo archives of the Iron Range Research and Interpretive Center.

[14] "Prize Winners in Various Events at Winter Carnival" and "Cold Wave Hits All Minnesota Tuesday Night," *Brainerd Tribune*, Jan. 17, 1935; "Frigid Weather Delays Carnival, Postponed Till Coming Week," *Brainerd Tribune*, Feb. 20, 1936.

[15] "Plans for Big Winter Sports Event Advance," *Bemidji Daily Pioneer*, Jan. 8, 1932; "Winter Sports Carnival Gets Started Today," *Bemidji Daily Pioneer*, Jan. 22, 1932.

[16] Art Lee and Rosemary Given Amble, "Paul Bunyan," in *Bemidji: First City on the Mississippi* (Bemidji: Privately printed, [1996]), 19.

[17] Lee and Amble, "Paul Bunyan," 18. Laughed's collection, *The Marvelous Exploits of Paul Bunyan* (Minneapolis: Red River Lumber Co., 1922), apparently included several logging camp figures and tales of his own invention. Representative collections outside the Midwest are *Paul Bunyan*, by Esther Shepherd (Seattle: McNeil Press, 1924), and the enduring bestseller, *Paul Bunyan*, by James Stevens (New York: Alfred A. Knopf, 1925).

[18] Lee and Amble, "Paul Bunyan," 19; "Carnival Getting Fine Publicity for Bemidji," *Bemidji Daily Pioneer*, Jan. 15, 1937.

[19] "Paul Bunyan Winter Carnival Program," *Bemidji Daily Pioneer*, Jan. 13, 1937; "Bunyan Winter Carnival Will Open Thursday," *Bemidji Daily Pioneer*, Jan. 12, 1938; "Program Tonight Centered in Municipal Sports Arena," *Bemidji Daily Pioneer*, Feb. 9, 1940.

[20] "Bunyan Winter Carnival Will Open Thursday," *Bemidji Daily Pioneer*, Jan. 12, 1938; "Paul Bunyan Winter Carnival Sidelights," *Bemidji Daily Pioneer*, Jan. 17, 1939; "Bemidji Ready to Entertain Thousands in Next Four Days," *Bemidji Daily Pioneer*, Jan. 18, 1939. The ice sculptors' specific niche in WPA programming is difficult to determine. The Federal Arts Project funded sculptural work done only with certain specified materials, and ice was not among them.

[21] "Sports Arena to Be Center of Carnival Activities Tonight," *Bemidji Daily Pioneer*, Jan. 20, 1939.

[22] *SPPP*, Photo Gravure Section, Feb. 3, 1935.

[23] Rolf Fjelstad, "Skating," typed manuscript in the *Minneapolis Journal* files, ca. 1936, special collections of Minneapolis Public Library; Connie Baker Wolfe, "Olympic Medalist Kenny Bartholomew Brings Silver Skates Races Back to Powderhorn," *Southwest Journal*, Dec. 1991.

[24] Fjelstad, "Skiing," typed manuscript in the *Minneapolis Journal* files, ca. 1936, special collections of Minneapolis Public Library.

[25] Fjelstad, "Skiing"; "World's Top Ski Slide to Be Erected Here," *SPPP*, Oct. 31, 1937.

[26] "City Splashed with Color for Parade Tonight," *SPPP*, Jan. 30, 1937. Wiggington signed presentation drawings and elevations of several of the ice castles built between 1937 and 1942, while Bassford's name appears only in the title block. On any account, Wiggington's role as chief designer in the city architect's office under Bassford's tenure has been well established.

[27] "Ex-King Recalls Parade Fiasco," *SPPP*, Feb. 2, 1942.

[28] "Music Master to Guide March in Auditorium," *SPPP*, Feb. 2, 1937; "Today's Program," *SPPP*, Jan. 30, 1937; "Vallee Bids Collegians to Good Time Tonight," *SPPP*, Feb. 1, 1937.

[29] "Watch Ski and Ice Marks Fall; 15,000 Children Parade Today," *SPPP*, Feb. 1, 1937.

30 "Boreas Crowned as Crowds Cheer" and "Year's Worst Cold Wave Grips N.W.," *SPPP*, Jan. 31, 1938.

31 "They Love a Parade — Risk Life and Limb for Vantage Points," *SPPP*, Jan. 29, 1939.

32 "Thousands Arrive to See Parade Opening Winter Carnival Today," *SPPP*, Jan. 28, 1939; "Carnival Program," *SPPP*, Jan. 29, 1939.

33 Linus Glotzbach, *WPA Accomplishments: Minnesota, 1935-1939* [St. Paul: WPA Administration of Minnesota, 1940]; "Map of Realm of Boreas Rex, the Capital Field of the Saint Paul Winter Carnival," *SPPP*, Jan. 22, 1939. Other carnival sources described the ski slide as an exact duplicate of the structure used in the 1936 Olympic games in Berlin. The two claims could both be correct.

34 "30,000 Will March Today in Biggest Carnival Parade," *SPPP*, Jan. 27, 1940; "Spectacle Billed as Best in History," *SPPP*, Feb. 2, 1941; "Carnival Week Packed with Entertainment," *SPPP*, Jan. 25, 1942.

35 "Carnival Week Packed with Entertainment," *SPPP*, Jan. 25, 1942; "Winter Carnival History," in *St. Paul Winter Carnival Program*, [1970]. The apparent incongruity of a national championship held after the international championship was probably due to the lack of organization of the sport on an international level. Any tournament could lay claim to be determining an international champion so long as champion skiers of more than one nation were present. National ski championships, on the other had, were officially sanctioned by the National Ski Association.

WINTER CELEBRATIONS TODAY (pp. 140-148)

1 "Winter Carnival History," St. Paul Winter Carnival Program, [1970]; Bob and Linda Fletcher and Jack and Mona LaMont, *St. Paul Centennial Ice Palace* (Privately published, 1986).

2 Bob and Linda Fletcher and Jack and Mona LaMont, *St. Paul Centennial Ice Palace* (Privately published, 1986); *The St. Paul Winter Carnival Pepsi Ice Palace Pictorial Souvenir Book* (St. Paul: Privately published, 1992). Even at an artistic level, St. Paul's ice castles offered little competion to the modernist fantasies erected in Quebec in the 1970s and the spectacular quasi-historical castles that rose in great numbers each year in Sapporo, Japan. See *Ice Palaces*, by Fred Anderes and Ann Agranoff (New York: Abbeville Press, 1983).

3 Conversation with Ken Bresley, Aug. 20, 1996; "A History of the Festival" and "Putting the Blame Where it Belongs: An Interview with Festival Organizers," *Pout-Independent*, Feb. 9, 1984. Pat Bauer and *Pilot-Independent* editor Paul Nye are also major contributors to eelpout lore.

SOURCES OF ILLUSTRATIONS

jacket front. T.W. Ingersoll photo; MHS
jacket back. Archives, St. Paul Heritage and Festival Foundation
half title page. Northeast Minnesota Historical Center
frontispiece. Bruce Christiansen
12. Elmer and Tenney photo; MHS
14. MHS
16. MHS
17. MHS
18t. *Harper's Weekly*; MHS
18b. MHS
19t. F. Scobie photo; MHS
19b. L.H. Halverson photo; MHS
20. Kenneth M. Wright photo; MHS
22. MHS
23. MHS
24. C.J. Greanleaf photo; MHS
25. MHS (color)
26. MHS
28. A.F. Burnham photo; MHS
29. B.F. Childs photo; International Museum of Photography, George Eastman House; MHS
30t. MHS
30b. Chester S. Wilson photo; MHS
31. MHS
32. S.C. Sargent photo; MHS
33. MHS
35. MHS
36. MHS
40. MHS
42. C.A. Zimmerman photo; MHS
43. C.A. Zimmerman photo; MHS
45. MHS
46t. T.W. Ingersoll photo; MHS
46b. MHS
48. MHS
49. MHS (color)
50. MHS (color)
51. *Frank Leslie's Illustrated Newspaper*; MHS
53. C.A. Zimmerman photo; MHS
54. C.A. Zimmerman photo; MHS
55. MHS
56. MHS (color)
57. MHS
58. MHS
59. MHS

60. MHS
61. MHS
62. H.H. Bennett photo; private collection
64. MHS (color)
65. MHS (color)
66. H.H. Bennett photo; MHS
67t. MHS
67b. MHS
68. Zimmerman and Ingersoll photo; MHS
69. Archives, St. Paul Heritage and Festival Foundation
70. C.A. Zimmerman and Ingersoll photo; MHS
71. MHS (color)
72t. T.W. Ingersoll photo; MHS
72b. T.W. Ingersoll photo; MHS
73. Ingersoll photo; MHS
74l. MHS
74r. C.A. Zimmerman photo; MHS
75. MHS (color)
76. MHS
77. MHS
78. MHS
79. *Harper's Weekly*; MHS
81. MHS
82. Hennepin History Museum
84. *Frank Leslie's Illustrated Magazine*; Wilson Library, University of Minnesota
85t. MHS (color)
85b. MHS
86. MHS
88. Pope County Historical Society
89. MHS (color)
90. MHS
91. Hennepin History Museum
92. MHS
93. MHS
94. MHS
95. MHS
96. Northeast Minnesota Historical Center
98t. New York Herald photo; MHS
98b. Archives, St. Paul Heritage and Festival Foundation
99t. Archives, St. Paul Heritage and Festival Foundation (color)
99b. MHS
100t. Camera Art Co. photo; Archives, St. Paul Heritage and Festival Foundation
100b. Archives, St. Paul Heritage and Festival Foundation
100r. Archives, St. Paul Heritage and Festival Foundation
101. MHS
102t. *St. Paul Dispatch* photo; MHS
102b. MHS
103. Camera Art Co. photo; Archives, St. Paul Heritage and Festival Foundation
104t. MHS (color)
104b. Camera Art Co.; Archives, St. Paul Heritage and Festival Foundation
105. Archives, St. Paul Heritage and Festival Foundation
106t. Archives, St. Paul Heritage and Festival Foundation
106b. St. Paul Winter Carnival photo; MHS
107. MHS

108. MHS
109t. MHS
109b. MHS
110t. World Wide photo; MHS
110b. Norton and Peel photo; Minneapolis Public Library
111. MHS
112. MHS
113. Northeast Minnesota Historical Center
114. MHS
115. MHS (color)
116t. *Minneapolis Journal* photo; MHS
116b. *Virginia Daily Enterprise* graphic; MHS
117. MHS
118. MHS
121. Minneapolis Public Library
122. Iron Range Research and Interpretive Center
123. Iron Range Research and Interpretive Center
124. MHS
125t. Beltrami County Historical Society
125b. Beltrami County Historical Society
126. Beltrami County Historical Society
127t. MHS
127b. MHS
128. MHS
129l. MHS
129r. Minneapolis Public Library
130. MHS
131l. Minneapolis Public Library
131r. MHS
132t. Minneapolis Public Library
132b. *Minneapolis Tribune* photo; MHS
133t. Archives, St. Paul Heritage and Festival Foundation
133b. MHS
134t. Robert Beveridge photo; MHS
134b. MHS
135t. Archives, St. Paul Heritage and Festival Foundation
135b. MHS
136l. MHS
136r. WPA photo; MHS
137t. MHS
137b. MHS
138l. Northeast Minnesota Historical Center
138r. Northeast Minnesota Historical Center
140. Minneapolis Public Library
142. MHS
143a. Minneapolis Public Library
143b. MHS
144. Archives, St. Paul Heritage and Festival Foundation
145. MHS
146t. St. Paul Carnival Association photo; MHS
146b. Paul Nye photo
146r. Voyageur Week Winter Festival
147. Voyageur Week Winter Festival
148. Paul Clifford Larson photo (color)

Original color images noted above have been reproduced without alteration.
Black and white photographs have been selectively tinted by the book designer,
Lois Stanfield, in much the same manner as archival tinted photographs.

DESIGNED BY LOIS STANFIELD

LIGHTSOURCE IMAGES

TYPEFACE IS BEMBO

ARCHIVAL BLACK & WHITE PHOTOS

COLORED BY DESIGNER

USING DIGITAL IMAGING SOFTWARE